Dear Motherhood

A catalogue record for this book is available from the National Library of New Zealand.

Soft cover ISBN 978-0-473-56872-6

Hard cover ISBN 978-0-473-56873-3

Kindle ISBN 978-0-473-56875-7

epub ISBN 978-0-473-56874-0

iBook ISBN 978-0-473-56876-4

Design & layout www.yourbooks.co.nz

Printed in New Zealand by www.yourbooks.co.nz

This book has been printed using sustainably managed stock.

Dear Motherhood

A collection of real, raw and romantic poetry and prose
about the big little love story that is early motherhood.

Sincerely

EMMA HEAPHY

This book is dedicated to my husband and children,
My main supporters and inspiration.
May they always be reminded of how much they mean to me, how much I've grown because of them and how many memories we have made together.

Contents

Introduction

Dearest Reader,

Welcome to my book of poetry and prose on early motherhood – a candid but heartfelt account of my experiences and learnings through the most difficult, yet beautiful, season.

Motherhood comes in many stages. Mothers come in different forms. What resonates with some mothers will not with others.

It is for this reason that Dear Motherhood is made up of chapters addressed to the different stages and forms of Mother I have lived. Each chapter is filled with musings to inspire, empower and provide comfort to those of you who are about to enter a certain stage, who are already in a certain stage or who want to remember a certain stage.

Motherhood can be a challenging and lonely road, the beauty of which can often be lost in it all. This book is your reminder that you are not alone in your journey and that the beauty is still there, even if some days it's hard to find.

So, who am I?

I am Emma – a qualified lawyer, overthinker and, since 2018, a Stay-at-Home Mother. We live a very rural life on a beef and sheep farm in New Zealand. When I am not tending to my littles, you will often find me writing; a passion that I have reignited since motherhood, that I have shared with the world via my social media channels and that now makes up the pages of this book of my story. But I am not your typical motherhood story and this not your typical motherhood book.

Motherhood made me, rearranged me and shaped me. What I thought was not something I was born to do, became the missing piece of my puzzle. What I subconsciously delayed starting, became something that I am frightened will someday come to an end. What I thought would leave me bored and dissatisfied, continues to give me the biggest sense of fulfilment.

My former life as a career-driven family lawyer was all I knew. Working long hours, pushing myself for monthly targets and focusing only on my career was my purpose, my passion, my life. The fast-paced nature of that life was intense but rewarding, and I became addicted to it. I thought I would continue to be as I fumbled my way through motherhood, but it wasn't like that at all.

The awkwardness, the lack of maternal instinct, the shame for not having a clue were all factors I thought would feature prominently in my motherhood experience. But I proved myself wrong.

The life I worried about became the life I had always craved. I found my feet. I found some form of balance. It came naturally, most of the time.

From the career woman who would not stop at anything to advance her goals, to the woman who would stop everything for the little hearts that filled hers, this is my journey through the early years of motherhood. May the poems and prose of my journey also speak to yours and be a source of inspiration, empowerment and validation for you when you need it most.

With love,

Emma.
xx

CHAPTER ONE

DEAR NON-MATERNAL WOMAN

Just because you do not like holding another woman's newborn, does not mean you are not born to be the mother of your own.

When is the right time?

Maternal was never something I thought I was. I was never "clucky", and holding someone else's baby never seemed to come naturally. It felt awkward and stressful. Every time I would jokingly preface the cuddle with "let's see how long they last before they cry" and when they cried in my arms, I would seriously think "see, I'm not made for this".

I believed that I was not cut out for motherhood and doubted with every inch of my being whether I would ever be able to give my own baby enough if and when that time came. When discussions were had about "trying", it made me nervous. For a while I hid behind my "career goals" to delay the process. When I got pregnant, I would joke with friends, family and work colleagues about how soon I would be back at work. I said 6–12 months, but sooner was what I envisaged. They were all ways of protecting myself from what I thought was going to be the inevitable struggle to connect with my baby once born. That was not my reality.

The moment I became a mother, I knew I was born for it. The love I had for my baby was limitless. The connection we had in the first moments was like nothing I had ever experienced. My chest was the only one she wanted to snuggle into. My arms were the only ones she wanted to cradle her. My scent was the only one that gave her comfort. There was no awkwardness, just a natural reaction to someone else's needs. There was no return to my former work, just a new lifestyle that has become my priority.

When I look back now, I wish I had known a few things. I wish I had known that one's motherhood journey cannot be predicted. I wish I had known that failing to connect with babies that were not my own was not a marker of a destined inability to connect with my own one day. I wish I had known that natural maternity can be born at the same time as your baby. Because this is what I know now, and hindsight can be a wonderful thing.

My awakening

Motherhood has forced me to slow down,
To walk at someone else's pace, without needing to rush my own.
To see the simple pleasures that life brings, rather than the ever-growing and complicated inbox.
To feel the pressure of tight little arms around me, not of monthly targets in my diary.
And I needed to.
It's a fast-paced world out there.
It's hard not to get caught up in it all and lose sight of what's right there.
But I did, often.
My awakening has been this season.
Where things remain unfinished, delays are inevitable and the pay check is love.
Where nothing makes sense a lot of the time, yet everything feels right.
Where I have been pushed and pulled every day since the beginning.
It's been the slowing I never knew I needed.
But I'm here now,
And it's all going so fast.

Please don't worry

To the woman reading this who doesn't feel ready to become a mother, don't worry. You may never feel ready but become ready.

To the woman who doesn't know whether she wants children at all, don't panic. You sometimes don't know what you want until you have it.

To the woman who is worried about what will happen to her career if she has children, don't let that stop you. You are allowed to have personal goals, mother or not.

To the woman who does not think she is cut out for motherhood, don't let that limit you. You will always be the perfect fit for your child.

To the woman who is feeling all or some of these feelings, don't feel alone. You have shared this experience with many women before you and around you.

To the mother who has felt all or some of these feelings before, don't feel guilty. You were not to know how motherhood would change you, rearrange you or shape you.

Woman, mother-to-be, mother, please don't worry.
You will be more than enough,
You are more than enough,
You will forever be more than enough,
Trust me.

CHAPTER TWO

DEAR PREGNANT WOMAN

Growing life is not meant to be easy,
but it is meant to be worth it.

The unglamorous

Pregnancy isn't always perfect bumps, soft skin, luscious locks and glows. It can be imperfect bumps, blemished skin and dead hair.

It isn't always glamorous or perfect or graceful. In fact, a lot of the time it can feel the opposite.

It can look like your head over the toilet bowl, trying to squirm awkwardly into compression tights and your torso oblivious to the state of your legs and toe nails, which are lost underneath.

You can have marks that weren't there before, hair in funny places and a constant heaviness that is not just a number on the scale.

And that's ok because pregnancy is not meant to be perfect, glamorous or graceful.
It is a process that requires change, sacrifice and growth.
Our bodies are not made of bricks and mortar.
They are made to adapt, to move, to evolve, and when it comes to pregnancy they do, quickly.

In only nine short months they create a new life from scratch. A life that relies solely on them for growth, nourishment and safety. It's no small feat.

So, we shouldn't expect anything more from them. We should just try to embrace the ungraceful, the unglamorous, the imperfect. Because at the end of the day, they are often just the by-products of a process. A process that creates a little end product who gives us far more than a few insecurities and sees us as nothing other than perfect.

The uneasy road

I get it.

I get how you can be absolutely exhausted during the day but restless at night.

I get how you can suddenly want to eat everything all at once but then touch nothing for hours.

I get how you can worry about everything one moment and then forget what you were worrying about the next.

I get how one day you can hardly feel pregnant but the next you can feel like you are carrying an elephant.

I get how you feel bad for not getting anything done but then worry that you have done too much.

I get how you want to be further on than you are but also enjoy every moment of growing new life.

I get how you feel self-conscious in clothes some days and then the proudest you have been in them the next.

I get that you want to socialise with your friends but that staying home in your PJs is often more appealing.

I get how you can wish some days away but then pine for your smaller bump days back.

I get how you can be emotionally steady one moment and then on a complete roller coaster the next.

I get how you can complain about how hard it can be but be incredibly grateful all at once.

I get it. Every bit of it. You are not alone.

While pregnancy is different for all women and each pregnancy can be different for one woman, we share in the experience together.
Together we are growing humans.
Our body is their home.
They take, we give.
It's not meant to be easy, but it is meant to be worth it,
Every single bit of it.

Focus shift

As a pregnant woman, and certainly as a soon-to-be new mum, it's easy to focus on the birth stories shared that can, at times, leave you feeling worried and somewhat fearful in the lead-up. Everyone talks about these.

However, when your mind is turned to it, what's even easier is noticing the number of mothers passing you with children in tow every day and remembering that every single one of them has successfully brought a child into the world.
This in itself can leave you feeling encouraged and empowered.
This is where the focus should be, and it takes just one person to turn your mind.

Overdue

Overdue Mama,

It's been a long wait, hasn't it?
The days are passing by at a snail's pace, and waiting for the clock
hand to reach a new hour is like watching paint dry.
You're tired and over being over it.
You thought they would be here by now,
But they're not.
And as you field calls and messages from others about their
arrival, only to tell them once again that nothing's changed, your
impatience grows.

I know you know,
You know they will be here in the next few days or weeks—they
have to be—but thinking that doesn't really make it any easier.
You just want them to be here now, to hold them, to see them, to
know that they are ok.

You know they will come when they are ready—of course they
will—but you have been ready for weeks now.
You have cleaned your home when it doesn't need it and have
rearranged your hospital bag too many times to count, just in case
today is the day.

You know you will be even more tired when they arrive, but that's a different sort of tired.
Not a tiredness of carrying them inside without the unknowns of what's to come, but a tiredness of carrying them with your arms, your eyes, every breath, knowing exactly how worth it it is.

You know that you should make the most of this last little window of opportunity to rest, read and go for walks, of your present before the change, but you struggle to muster the energy.
Walking can be painful, lying down is uncomfortable and being in the present is just not that enjoyable anymore.

I know you're trying to move things along naturally, to avoid this current scenario, but nothing is working and you are now questioning yourself.
You wonder if your dates are wrong, whether you could have done something differently, and doubt your intuition that fed you a much different story earlier.

Overdue Mama,
I know you know,
Because I know too.
I know it's hard, it seems unfair and it's testing you.
I know you feel bad about complaining and venting, but can't help it.
I know you're beyond grateful and excited for what's to come, but sometimes the current wait consumes you.

But I also know,
And I know you know it too,
That it's better late than never.

Dear a new Mum

Dear a new Mum,

Here is what I want you to know:

You will be the most tired you have ever been, but your tiredness
will be overtaken by the deepest love you have ever felt.
Rise.
Sleep.
Rise.
Every missed minute of sleep is worth it.

You will have no idea what you are doing, but you will know
exactly what your child needs.
Doubt.
Intuition.
Doubt.
Every doubt is answered by your intuition.

You will feel weighed down by others opinions, but that weight is
lifted when you realise it is only your opinion your child cares for.
This way.
That way.
This way.
Every way needs to be your way.

You will mourn your pre-baby life sometimes, but that is quickly forgotten when you see your child smile.
You miss her.
You love her.
You miss her.
Every smile confirms you are exactly where you need to be.

You will have your bad days, but the good days make the bad a distant memory.
Bad day.
Good day.
Bad day.
Every good day is worth ten of the bad ones.

You will miss having as much time for just you, but the time that is shared will bring you the most joy.
You want a break.
You miss them.
You want a break.
Every sacrifice is for a love like no other.

You will feel self-conscious a lot, but to your child you are beautiful just the way you are.
You would change that.
You love that.
You would change that.
Everyone who understands will not judge.

You will have less time with your partner, but spending time as a family becomes what you crave.
All of you.

Just us.
All of you.
Every moment spent without your child feels a little empty.

You will be tested more than ever, but those tests come with the best rewards.
Cries.
Love.
Cries.
Every hug, smile and new word becomes your proudest moment.

Motherhood is full of contradictions, but that's why it's so beautiful.
You have a lot to look forward to.
It's an incredible ride.

Dearest child,

newly born

We both gasp for air. You breathing in the new world around you, me trying to regain my strength.

We both shed emotion. You shrieking as you find your voice in my arms, me weeping out the relief that you are here.

We both crawl closer. You leading with your nose up my chest, me with my lips down to the top of your head.

We both then rest. You nuzzled under my neck, me under your steadying rise and fall.

And there we both stay,
Separate but more connected than ever,
As we are both newly born.

Worth it

I waited and waited for you,
For nine whole months.
Since the beginning which felt so rough,
Through the middle which felt like a teaser,
To the end which felt so long.
My patience was tested in every way,
But you were worth the wait,
To me, you are perfect.

I worried and worried over you,
About everything that could go wrong.
Whether I could give you what you need,
Whether you would enter this world healthy,
Whether we would continue our journey after we met.
My worry for you was constant,
But you were worth every worry,
You are my everything.

I tossed and turned every night for you,
Looking for the comfort I craved.
Trying so hard to rest because I was tired,
Fighting insomnia like it was something I could control,
Waking to your movements because I wanted to check on you.
My darkness was more awake than asleep,

But you were worth every sleepless night,
You are what I dreamed of.

I've stretched and stretched some more for you.
In every which way imaginable.
My body was pulled and scarred,
My mind was opened wider,
My heart was torn throughout.
My give knew no bounds,
But you were worth every stretch,
You are the growth worth celebrating.

I've pushed and pushed my body to get you here,
It's not always been easy.
I endured physical intensity and exhaustion,
I tapped into every emotion possible,
I depleted most sources available.
I forgot just how testing it was,
But you were worth every push,
You are the result I'll remember.

I've given everything and more to be with you,
But it was so worth it.
My darling,
You were so worth it.

Your own

You were part of me,
You were part of him,
But you were never ours.

You have parts from me,
You have parts from him,
But you are your own.

You feel part of me,
You feel part of him,
But you will always be you.

You are part of me,
You are part of him,
But you will forever be yours.

CHAPTER THREE

DEAR POSTPARTUM MOTHER

*Focus on what your body has done for you,
not on what it hasn't done for your wardrobe.*

Aftermath

I felt the breath of him all over my skin.
I felt every inch of him soaked into my pores.
I felt at one with every part of him.
And it was beautiful.
But the bits that came with that?
Not always.

I felt the tired stuck to every part of me as I rolled out of bed again
and it wasn't even 5am.
I felt the sting from birthing and nourishing him, over every inch
of my body with every move I made.
I felt the milk that was missed clinging to the edges of my skin
and his little fingernails scratched into my chest.
I felt the discomfort of the padding, while it was catching the
aftermath of growing him.
I felt the emptiness of my stomach with my hands now full of
skin, my body now older but new.
I felt almost lifeless as I was about to start my day giving life to
him and his sister on an empty tank full of heart.

It was day six postpartum.
And I felt the aftermath more than ever.
I felt so in love, but so in need of a moment for myself.
To process and reflect on the new.

So I showered.
Not for the first time since birth, but for the first time in 24 hours.
And it was everything.

The tiredness seemed to wash away with the weight of being so
needed and the stings became lesser.
I felt my new skin and watched the droplets of water move
differently over it. It still formed shapes and they were beautiful.
I felt the weight of the aftermath fall off me, leaving only the smell
of him on every part of me. That scent could never be washed
away. I didn't want it to be either.

And afterwards I felt him again.
I held him close to me.
And we carried on with our day.
I felt like a new woman, ready for the hard bits to wash over me
again.

This is what helped me survive early postpartum.
By taking a shower when I could.
By washing away the sting.
By freshening up my perspective.
By cleansing the parts of me that needed cleansing.

Because postpartum is a big thing to go through.
It's important.
It's the aftermath, but it shouldn't be an afterthought.
It's about trying not to get washed away completely sometimes.
And sometimes it's the littlest things that can make the biggest
difference,
Like a shower.

Bare

There is something so beautiful about a mother in her natural state.

No makeup, imperfect hair, dark half-moons cratering underneath her eyes and the little wings that emerge on each side of her face that have been formed from the endless smiles she has worn since bringing life into the world.

The dressing gowns she wears for comfort during the long days and nights, the older clothes that are stained with her child's little fingerprints and the confidence she wears when breastfeeding her baby without covering up.

Every part of her reflects what she is living. It's a raw and real beauty that tells a story.

However, sometimes it's hard to see this beauty in ourselves in a world where beauty seems to be defined by perfection.
We apologise for the way we look to others, as if it is something to be ashamed of.
"I'm sorry, I'm looking like a mess today."
"I'm sorry, I haven't had time to do my makeup."
"I'm sorry, I'm embarrassed you are seeing me like this."

Our natural state is not something to apologise for, ever! It is something to be proud of and own. It is beautiful in every way, not just "in its own way".

Beauty is in the eye of the beholder, it's true.
As women and mothers, we therefore need to be unapologetically confident in our beauty in all forms, for ourselves and for our children.

Bouncing forward

I looked in my wardrobe for something to wear.
I tried on a few of my older dresses, then T-shirts, then jeans.
Soon they were all lying in a pile on the floor around me.
And so was my confidence.

I'm a size or two up from where I used to be, and things just don't
fit, let alone fit the same. So I went for my baggy linen T-shirt and
maternity jeans combo. These are my safe options, my go-tos, my
"every day when I'm leaving the house" staples right now.
They make me feel comfortably confident.

But it seemed like such a waste.
A waste of these clothes of mine in that pile.
The clothes that are now too small and make me feel now too big.
Those clothes that waste space in my wardrobe and waste away at
my confidence.
And I know this, I do.
This truth is not wasted on me.

Yet I still keep them, all of them, in the hope that one day I might
fit back into them exactly as I used to.
In the hope that the pile on the floor will be no longer.
In the hope that my confidence is picked up and worn with them.
And it's hopeless.

But this is what we are so often fed as women postpartum.
That bouncing back is the goal.
That getting back to where we were before we became a mother or before we had our second or third or fourth child is the golden standard.
That fitting back into those old jeans without a wrestle is worthy of unnecessary space in our minds and wardrobes.
And it's unhealthy.

Is it not a potential outcome that I may never get back to the same size I was?
Or that my body isn't meant to fit back into those dresses and tops and jeans exactly like it used to?
Or that maybe, just maybe, my body has changed because of what it's been through and my mindset needs to as well?

We need to be fed this as part of the postpartum diet more.
We need to be encouraged to part with the old clothes more.
We need to be told to wrestle less and size up more.
We need to normalise "bouncing forward", not "bouncing back".

Because confidence should not come from what size we wear, but who we are.
And while we may get back to what size we were, we also may not.
And this seems to be a much healthier starting point.
From where I'm sitting anyway.

Through their eyes

I needed to pop into the supermarket. I was wearing my "I hope I don't see anyone" attire. My matted hair was hidden under a cap, my sunglasses remained on for as long as possible and my milk-stained top from breastfeeding in the front seat was disguised by a sweatshirt I found in the boot. I felt distressed at the thought of someone seeing me. But I had to go. I needed baby wipes. Why is it always the baby wipes?

I put him in the capsule holder and around the supermarket we went. I was in a rush. I didn't want to be seen. And my main focus was scanning the area in front for known oncoming traffic.

We got to the baby aisle, finally. I was relieved that I hadn't seen anyone yet or rather, that no one had seen me.
I spotted the wipes and pushed the trolley past a lady stocking the shelf. I think I smiled at her in my haste. I hope I did. I can't remember.

As I reached for the wipes, I heard her say, "he hasn't taken his eyes off you".
I turned to her and she repeated it once more, with a smile.
I smiled back. I know I did. It was a memorable moment.
Then I turned to him. And sure enough,
his big beady eyes were locked on me.

And as ours met, he smiled as if to say, "Mum, seeing you makes me happy".

And there was a shift, a beautiful realisation that I was perfect to him exactly as I was. That my matted, milk-stained, self-conscious self was all he could see, all he wanted to see.
And I had missed that, when I was too busy desperately trying to have that version of myself missed by others.
It seemed so silly in retrospect.
It always does.

So we took our time for the rest of the shop. And my main focus was him as we scanned the aisles for other things I needed but hadn't wanted to waste time on earlier.
We smiled a lot, we cooed and I was relaxed.
I didn't see anyone, but it wouldn't have worried me if I had, not then.
I had been reminded that someone sees the beauty in me, even if I can't.
And that had given me perspective.

Sometimes we just need to see things from a different view, like from behind the beady little eyes that never leave us,
Even if we need to be reminded to by a stranger in the supermarket.

Thank goodness for the baby wipes.

As you are

Dear Mum,

If I could tell you what I am thinking, this is what I would say.

You don't like the varicose veins on your legs which worsened when you grew me. You wear pants to hide them, even when it's too hot. I wouldn't notice them if you didn't tell dad about them all the time. I'm too busy trying to catch your smile. I love your legs just the way they are.

You don't like that your arms are bigger than they used to be. Your arms are nice and strong so you can carry me each day. I can't walk and I rely on you to help me get to where I need to go. I love your arms just the way they are.

You think your boobs are less perky than they used to be. Your boobs fed me for months and have been my comfort when I have felt worried or scared. I love your boobs just the way they are.

You think your tummy is squishier than it used to be. Your tummy grew me for nine months just so I could be here today. It's soft like a cushion and makes me feel comfortable when I am cuddling into you. I love your tummy just the way it is.

You don't like that you can't fit in to some of your old jeans. I don't know what size you used to be and that doesn't matter to me anyway. I love you just the way you are now.

You don't like the new stretch marks on your body. You say they are the reason you don't like going swimming at the beach. You sit wrapped in your towel watching instead. Please come swimming. Please come and enjoy me as I am and let me enjoy you as you are. I love your stretch marks just the way they are.

Mum, just so you know,
You are the most beautiful thing I have ever seen.
You are all I ever see.
And I would not change one single thing about you.
Because I love you,
Just the way you are.

Dearest child,

You are my reason

You are the reason I get up each morning.
Even though my eyelids are as heavy as a five-tonne truck.
Even though all I want is a sleep in, a coffee and breakfast in bed.
You are more important.
You need me.
For you, I would do anything.

You are the reason I am finally comfortable in my own skin.
Even though I am a size bigger than I used to be.
Even though my boobs cannot be described as "perky".
You relied on my body.
You gave it purpose.
For you, I will always love it.

You are the reason I am no longer selfish.
Even though I sometimes complain that I don't buy anything for myself anymore.
Even though I get annoyed when I don't get enough alone time.
You have taught me that there is more to life than just me.
Your needs come first right now.
For you, I happily come second.

You are the reason I now know the importance of patience.
Even though I sometimes miss the fast-paced life.
Even though I still get frustrated when I feel inefficient.
You need me to go at your pace.
You are the priority right now.
For you, I slow down.

You are the reason that I now have perspective.
Even though I don't make the money that I used to.
Even though I don't have the level of mental stimulation I once
had.
You are more important.
You need me.
For you, my career can wait.

You are the reason I worry more than ever.
Even though I know it won't change anything.
Even though it's not your fault.
You are precious.
You are vulnerable.
For you, I will worry forever.

You are the reason I am now filled with gratitude.
Even though I get sad when things do not go my way.
Even though I sometimes lose sight of what I have.
You are my constant reminder that I am blessed.
You are the light at the end of every tunnel.
For you, everything is worth it.

You are the reason that my heart is full.
Even though I love your dad more than you can ever imagine.

CHAPTER THREE

Even though I am grateful for our life before you.
You have shown me a love like no other.
You are remarkable.
For you, my heart explodes.

Chapter
Four

Dear Newborn Mother

They are newly born, but so are you, into a new role that you have no training for. Give yourself some grace.

A new everything

I remember the final day in hospital with my first. So tired, but the freshest I'd been in days, following the first hair-wash post birth. You couldn't wipe the smile off my face. She was perfect to us. Things could not have felt more perfect either. And as we walked through the hospital doors into the world with her on our own, we were very much on our own too.

People don't really talk about the period after birth much. The period where visitors come and go. There can be many. And it's lovely, but also tiring. Because despite how much help you get, and how much you appreciate their support, it's still on you.
Your baby wants you, not them. And being wanted and needed in this way, for the first time in your life, is wonderfully breathtaking. Make no mistake. But it's also exhausting, and at times debilitating.

Post birth you are tired. It's an exhausting ordeal no matter how it occurs. Your body needs time to recover, but there's no time. Not really. It's all go from the moment they enter the world.

You have to feed them. And regardless of how you feed them, you're waking every few hours or less.
You have to resettle them, regardless of how long it takes, and what that means for your own sleep.

You have to learn what works for them, and deal with what everyone says you should try or worked for them.

And it's the emotional toll of all these things, as much as it is the physical. It's the newness of everything. Your body, your baby, your life. It's dealing with things working and not working. It's your hormones. It's loving them so much you want to watch them every minute, but being so tired from being the only one they want every minute of every hour.

So, to the postpartum mum, first time or not, I'm not here to tell you to sleep when the baby sleeps or to make the most of any support you have. I'm just here to say that I know it can be a lot to be someone's everything. I know you can feel on your own no matter the support. And I know the smiles will be wiped off at times, and things will seem less than perfect.
Because that's all I wanted to hear.
And I've been there, twice.

Sincerely newborn

Dear Newborn Mother,

Please know that this is what productivity looks like.

It looks like feeding your baby on the couch for an hour, sometimes more.

It looks like leaving a dent in the cushions when you leave, if you leave, but you don't have to leave.

It looks like being constantly relied upon, and pooed on and spewed on.

It looks like burping them and cleaning them. And then cleaning yourself, but only if you have time.

It looks like ignoring the mess surrounding you and somehow making more. There is always more.

It looks like staring at them for the longest time so that you completely lose track of time.

It looks like taking lots of photos and videos of them and then cringing at the sound of your own voice on playback.

It looks like conversing in one-sided baby language and constantly thinking "there's a smile" with only the slightest of mouth movements.

It looks like stroking their hair, nuzzling them and kissing their cheeks because you still can't believe they are real.

It looks like asking your husband to bring you things. And not bring you things. And then him forgetting to bring you things.

It looks like rocking them, hushing them and singing to them. Or just anything that works really.

It looks like letting them fall asleep on you and letting them stay asleep on you.

It looks like putting them in their bassinet so you can sleep, but staring at them again instead.

It looks like you sleeping, eating and showering when you can. Or at least trying to anyway.

It looks like doing what you need to survive the days and nights, the weeks and months.

It looks like you and them, figuring it all out together, one day at a time.

Productivity comes in many different forms and this is one of them.

So, if you have done nothing other than some of the above today,
Know that you have been productive.
Know that you are working hard.
Know that you are doing great things.

You may not feel alive right now, but you are keeping someone else alive.
That's productivity at its finest.
Keep up the good work.

Best (sleep) wishes,
Another Newborn Mother.

She is the one

When all is dark outside,

She is the one.

Who fumbles for her phone and dressing gown, her eyes still closed;

Who moves with urgency to the noise, arms stretched out in front, feet dragging behind;

Who sits beside the cot, the bed, or in the feeding chair whispering softly, still finding her voice;

Who walks laps while carrying the load around the room, little hands reaching for her face, little feet trying to touch the ground;

Who faces the light of the screen, mindlessly scrolling, while trapped by the weight of life lying across or beside her;

Who moves from room to room, trying to meet the echoes of those little hearts who pine for her, her own beating with urgency;

Who tries desperately to get back to sleep when all is silent, her mind moving at pace, her eyes fully awake;

Who is dragged into the day sooner than she imagined, playing, reading and tending under the living-room lights, all before the birds start chirping.

Who is the one?

She is mother.

Enlightened

This won't be a pretty poem or piece of prose.
I don't have the energy for that today. Truth be told, I can hardly string two sentences together, let alone rhyme.
But I want to capture this moment and share my thoughts around it because sometimes, just sometimes, it's in the very moment that we can truly understand how we are feeling at the core.

In this very moment at the core I am feeling exhausted. I am feeling irritable. I am feeling moody.
I am feeling like I could cry at the drop of a hat, or explode, or literally fall asleep standing up.
The gas cylinder has been beeping for what seems like hours. It all seems so loud. I just want it to stop. Please stop.
I can't find anything I need, and it's making me frustrated, more frustrated than normal.
And I have almost no patience for the big emotions, mine included.

But here we are.
This is what happens when you have broken sleep, when you're sleep deprived, when you're in early motherhood.
This is real.
This is candid.
This is normal.

It's not every day that I feel like I could fall into my coffee cup,
but today is one of those days.
And I'm reminded that I've been here before and got through it.
That tomorrow will be different.
That it gets easier.
And this is true.

But I want to acknowledge that in this moment doing things on
little sleep, and broken sleep and anything but sleep is hard.
And I want to acknowledge that it is hard because sleep is a basic
human need, like food and water are.
And I want to acknowledge that at the core, it is what we require
to function, let alone function well.

I want to acknowledge these things because right now I'm being
hard on myself for feeling this way.
And it becomes harder than it should be.
And it's not fair, on me or them.

So today I remind myself it's not about doing all the things, but
doing the basics.
Because without the "basics", including sleep, it's not fair to expect
anything more of myself.
And at a basic level, which is all I can consider right now,
I'm relieved.
Because I'm cutting myself some slack,
Because I'm giving myself some grace,
Because I'm being realistic.

And it's (en)lightened me,
Right down to the core.

Fed is best

Latches,
Awkward holds,
Waking up in chest puddles,
Which side was last?
Leaks,
Hiding in public,
Covering up,
Is that a standard drink?
Expressing,
Frozen snap-lock bags,
Milk bar, ALWAYS open, draining.

These are just some of the things I think of when remembering the
start of my breastfeeding journey with my first.
I chose to breastfeed,
I was able to breastfeed,
My daughter was able to latch,
It just worked for us.
So this is what we did for eight months.

Feeding wherever,
Less awkward,
More efficient,
No covering up,

Expired frozen pouches,
Teeth,
Drained,
A night out?
More teeth,
Please take the bottle,
Independence, I'm ready, NOW.

These are just some of the things I think of when remembering the
end of our breastfeeding journey.
I chose to stop breastfeeding at eight months,
My daughter would have kept going,
I felt guilty about stopping,
I just wanted some of my independence back.
So to the bottle we went exclusively for months thereafter.

Feeding to sleep,
One-on-one time,
Connection,
Attachment,
Nourishment,
Care,
Beauty,
Love,
With breastfeeding, with bottle feeding, with both.

These are the important things I think of when remembering my
entire feeding journey.
I am grateful that I got to experience both.
I am grateful that my daughter got to experience both.
Both methods are different,

But they each provide what matters.

Everyone's experience is different.
Everyone's reasons are different.
Everyone's story is different.

Here's to less judgement.
Here's to more support.
Here's to "fed is best!"

Know this

Dear Mama,

I see you.

Underneath the dark bags that hang from your eyes, the deep wrinkles in your forehead and the untidy messy bun that sits on the top of your head, you are plagued with self-consciousness.

Between the messy unvacuumed floor, the unmade beds and the basket full of washing, you feel like you are in a constant state of overwhelm.

Amidst the endless painful cries, the public tantrums and the unruly broken sleep, you pray for things to get easier.

Amongst the constant external pressure, the unhelpful opinions and the personal challenges, you crave approval and validation.

But know this.

To your child, you are the most beautiful thing they have ever laid eyes on, and to everyone else, you are a natural reminder of the amazing sacrifices you make.

The state of your house does not define you. It is just a stage that will pass, and before long you will desperately pine for this time back again.

You are currently doing the hardest job you will ever do. Vocalising the struggles is healthy and should not be discouraged.

Doubt is unfair and unkind. It doesn't matter the source from which it derives, you must not let it win. Trust your decisions and believe in yourself always.

Triggered

Those first few months,
Triggered by a photo.

The difficulty we had deciding who would hold her triggers
memories of trying to find our groove as a team when we had no
idea what positions we were playing in.
The disagreements about how to hold her, whether we should have
taken the pram, whether she was too hot, too cold or needing
another nap.

The worrisome facial expressions as she was passed between us
triggers memories of playing in front of a crowd for the first time.
The anxiety about someone else wanting to hold her when we
hardly knew them, about her crying inconsolably in our arms
or about her being woken in the pram by someone wanting to
"just take a peep", all while trying to be "relaxed" and not "overly
protective" parents.

The awkwardness in general triggers memories of having to
practise new skills daily, which always took time to learn. Taking
ten hours to get her into her car seat for the first time and a
further ten to get the car temperature just right before our first
trip home from the hospital. Worrying about driving with her
for weeks afterwards and then driving at 30 km consistently no

matter the speed limit. Covering myself up while breastfeeding in a discreet corner while trying to get her latched in public.

The breastfeeding dress I wore triggers memories of suddenly having to account for and to a tiny coach with every decision we made as players. The extra time taken to get out of the door due to leaking breast pads, nappy explosions or sick down my freshly washed top. The decision to stay home rather than meet friends because she was being fussy or trying to find my credit card in my disorganised baby bag while keeping her asleep in my arms in front of a massive line behind me.

It all seems like a distant memory, but it's not. The journey through the parenthood game is quick. You learn and adapt quickly, almost as quickly as your child does.
They want you to play your best for them, to listen to them and to take the lead on the field.
And you do, every day.

We may not have won medals, but we sure have come so far as a team.
Oh those first few months.

Dearest child,

Torn by a sleepy newborn

Please don't wake, not yet,
There's more I need to do,
Like the washing, the dishes, and dinner,
Just to name a few.

Please don't wake, not yet,
There's more time before you're due,
For me to shower, change, brush my teeth,
We normally have till 2.

Please don't wake, not yet,
There's more I want to get done,
Like drink my coffee, read, paint my nails,
My new type of one-on-one.

Please don't wake, not yet,
There's someone I need to see,
About nothing, and everything, uninterrupted,
It's your dad, ok, it's he.

Please don't wake, not yet,
There's nothing at all to miss,
The dog barking, the car tooting, loudly,
It's all for nothing, I promise.

Please don't wake, not yet,
There's nowhere you need to be,
Not Plunket, baby group, my appointment,
Just asleep at home with me.

Please don't wake, not yet,
There's something I like to do,
Hear you breathe, catch you dream, see you relaxed,
It's peaceful watching you.

Please don't wake, not yet,
A few more things and I'm done,
Scroll through photos, videos and albums,
All of you, every one.

Please wake up, wake now,
There's something I need to say,
I love you, I missed you, let's cuddle,
My heart is torn, ok?

Good baby

People ask me whether you're a good baby.
And if I'm honest that question irks me a little.
Even though it's meant with the most love, it just doesn't sit right
with me.

You see,
You can be a good sleeper.
And you're a good feeder a lot of the time.
And you're good at cuddling, and smiling, and making life easy
for me most of the time.
Is that what people mean by good?
I guess it is,
By their standards.

But you also sometimes have unsettled nights.
And at the start your latch was slightly awkward.
And you sometimes cry, can be fussy, and want nothing I'm trying
to give.
Is that what other people mean by not so good?
I guess it is,
By their standards.

But guess what.
I'm not other people.
I'm your mum.
And the only standard I have is whether you are human.
Because regardless of size and age we are all human.

Being human is having good and bad moments.
It's feeling different emotions daily, sometimes all at once.
It's doing our best with what we know and the tools we have at the time, at any given time.

At your stage, it means trying to sleep without me sometimes when you don't know how, crying to communicate because you can't talk yet, and fussing when things feel too big for you.

At my stage, it means showing up for you no matter how tired I am, trying to read your wants and needs no matter how hard, and just generally trying no matter what.

Neither of us will always get it right.
And when we don't, we should not be defined as good or not so good.
Because moments are moments.
They pass.

So just so you know,
To me, you are not a good or not-so-good baby.
You are a little human who has good and bad moments,
Just like I do.

To me, you are more than a moment, or a series of moments,
So much more.

To me, you are perfect.
Exactly as you are,
Exactly as you do,
Exactly as you be,
Good and not so good, perfect and not so perfect, moments
included.

Learning together

It's not just you that's learning. It's the two of us learning together.

You learn I'm your safe place, while I learn to protect.

You learn to latch, while I learn to breastfeed.

You learn to take a bottle, while I learn to relax.

You learn to eat solids, while I learn to eat crusts.

You learn to talk, while I learn a new language.

You learn to crawl, while I learn to be alert.

You learn to smile, while I learn the best kind of warmth.

You learn to cry, while I learn a new pain.

You learn to cuddle, while I learn to hold on.

You learn to walk, while I learn to chase.

You learn to be away, while I learn to trust.

You learn to self-settle, while I learn resilience.

You learn to laugh, while I learn to be your clown.

You learn to adapt, while I learn to let go.

We both learn together and grow together.
Every day.
Every step of the way.

CHAPTER FIVE

DEAR TODDLER MOTHER

It is not called the terrible twos for no reason.
May your coffee be strong and your patience even stronger.

Toddler hold-ups

Getting out of the house with a toddler looks like…
Putting your alarm on the night before.
Waking earlier to another alarm (not the electronic version).
Getting up.
Putting your dressing gown on.
Not looking in the mirror.
Getting your toddler up.
Cuddling.
Consoling.
Cuddling.
Changing toddler's nappy.
Making toddler's breakfast.
Making your own coffee.
Feeding toddler breakfast.
Forgetting about your own coffee.
Reheating.
Tending to tantrum.
Giving toddler the toy thrown on top of the table during a
tantrum, which is now out of reach, to avoid a further tantrum.
Does NOT work.
Picking toddler up.
Cuddling.
Consoling.
Cuddling.

Tummy rumbling.
Remembering to eat.
Putting toast in toaster.
Hearing cat screech.
Removing toddler from cat.
Looking at time.
Panicking.
Late!
Getting toddler changed.
Preparing snacks.
Preparing baby bag.
Brushing teeth.
Looking in mirror.
Remembering...
Haven't got changed.
Haven't done hair.
Haven't had breakfast.
Haven't had coffee.
Getting self changed.
Interruption.
Picking up toilet rolls scattered around feet below.
Looking at time.
Very late!
Forgetting hair.
Forgetting toast.
Forgetting coffee.
Packing car.
*Insert first buckle sound here.
Giving toddler snacks.
Giving toddler toys.
Quietness.

**Insert second buckle sound here.
Still quietness.
Relief.
Taking first breath.
Grizzles start.
Turning on radio.
Seeing the time.
Remembering...
Still late.
Still hungry.
Still tired.
Still only 7.45am.

Peeves to pines

Finger smudges on the mirrors;
Toilet paper roads through the house;
"Mum mum mum" on repeat;
Muddy footprints on the carpet;
Crayon marks on the walls;
Pot-plant dirt sprinkled on the porch;
The clang of wooden spoons and pots;
Little fingers in my meal;
Clean socks worn outside;

But wait there's more.

Puddles in the kitchen;
Missing pages in my book;
Food stains on my top;
My underwear sprawled throughout the house;
LEGO in my coffee;
Soft toys in the bath;
The remote control always missing;
Sweeping piles destroyed;
Crumbs in the car seat;

But wait there's more.

Pegs all over the lawn;
Toilet rolls down the toilet;
Baby wipes everywhere in sight;
Cat food in milk bottles;
Ripped newspaper in the bed;
Spoons in the vege garden;
Makeup brushes in the dog bowl;
Honey fingers on the television screen;
My iPhone storage always full.

There is always more with toddlers,
And there is always a different more as they grow through
childhood.
Until one day there is no more,
And all you can do is wait for them to visit.

Puddle of emotions

There we were at 5pm on the kitchen floor. Tap running, potatoes boiling over and the bath routine waiting.

Everything stopped, as it does when this sort of thing happens. The thing that happens when you least expect and when you have the least energy.

The sort of thing this time was the sippy cup, which didn't have its usual orange lid. To me, it wasn't a big deal. I didn't think she would notice. It was just a sippy cup after all.
But boy oh boy, did she notice and boy oh boy did it become a big deal,
For us both.

What started with a few tears and attempted distraction tactics soon became turning the kitchen cupboards upside down and our emotions inside out.
She was trying to tell me, I was trying to listen, but neither of us could understand.
She couldn't understand why I couldn't find the right-coloured lid. I couldn't understand why blue wouldn't do. And in the moment neither of us could understand the gravity of what we were each feeling.

We both needed to sit, and breathe and regroup for a second. I needed to take the lead on that. I should have. But I didn't. It's always so clear in hindsight.

The thing is, despite what you know you should do, sometimes tantrums beat you both. They beat the one who has them and the one who witnesses them. They can feel completely out of control, and so can you. And sometimes you do lose control of your usually calm tone. You don't mean to, but you do. Because you're human.

In the heat of the moment it's easy to focus on how difficult you're making it for each other. But when the dust settles and you embrace one another on the kitchen floor, you tune in together and realise everything will be ok. Everything will be more than ok. Actually, your current is all that matters.
Not the lid colour or the imperfect parenting episode, just the two of you being there for each other as you navigate this sometimes-testing chapter together.

So here's to you,
The mother and toddler embracing each other's subsiding distress and growing calm on the kitchen floor, beside the cot or in the changing room at the mall.
You got there.
It may not have been your best moment,
But you're both doing your best.

Reminder to self

I don't always sleep through the night. I wake with worry, or when I have bad dreams, get thirsty, or am too hot or cold.

I don't always get to sleep easily. I think about the day, can't get comfortable, and sometimes need a cuddle.

I don't like it when the show I'm watching is stopped abruptly by a power cut, or a battery shortage. I feel hard done by, annoyed and frustrated.

I don't always like the meals I am served even if I think I feel like them beforehand. They don't always satisfy my cravings, can be too spicy or need more salt.

I don't like it when I can't find my favourite top to wear, book to read or cup to drink from. I often NEED to find these things NOW.

I never like being told I can't do something I want to do. Normally I protest and try to do it anyway.

So how can I expect anything more from them?
They can't even talk yet.

Littleness

Little eyes longing for me,
When she's meant to be asleep.

Little toes peeping under curtains,
When we play hide and seek.

Little ears burning hot,
When there's mention of Peppa Pig.

Little arms waving everywhere,
When she hears a catchy jig.

Little fingers meddling tirelessly,
When mixing what I'm yet to bake.

Little socks soaked thoroughly,
When I'm religiously running late.

Little tears streaming like rivers,
When she wants me to stay.

Little grizzles sending signals,
When she doesn't get her way.

Little hands tapping empty spaces,
When she wants me by her side.

Little fingernails digging into me,
When she's scared but cannot hide.

Little giggles filling our home,
When I knock my shin again.

Little smiles shining brightly,
When my eyes feel like rain.

Little by little she'll edge away,
When I'm still catching up.

Little by little she'll need me less,
When I'll still want to be stuck.

Little things are everything now,
When time is moving so fast.

Little will not exist forever,
When every first has a last.

Letting go

The sentences are starting to form
And the outfits are becoming her pick,

The doors are starting to slam
And the TV is on with a flick.

The eyes have started to veer
And the boots are on the right feet,

The questions are starting to flood
And "hi you" is her way to greet.

The day naps have started to end
and nights are more consistent,

The tantrums are starting to lessen
But the demands are more persistent.

The ears are starting to listen
And the movements are in reflect,

The requests include basic manners
But my mash is never "puuurfect".

The steps have started to fasten
Family names she can now list,

Toy collections have started to grow
And skipped pages are never missed.

Quiet time is starting to happen
But the Wiggles are her favourite band,

The clings are starting to loosen
Yet cups are held with one hand.

The showers have started to lengthen
Any help offered is answered "I can",

The independence has started to feature
And so early in her lifespan.

The new starts are coming in thick
And the ends are here just as fast,

It's hard to keep up with it all
It's like I'm living in the past.

All I can do is start letting go
And watch her starting the new,

While holding on to what she allows
Especially the hugs, which seem few.

Because that's what parenting is
It's helping them start starting now,

It's guiding them to independence
And letting go before knowing how.

Dear Mother of Girls,

Growing up

This is how I want you to grow up.
In a happy home, a loving home, a safe home;
Smiling when you're happy, crying when you're sad and yelling
when you're mad;
I want you to be able to feel emotion, understand emotion and
express emotion.

This is how I want you to grow up.
Learning through mess, learning through play and learning
through challenges;
Having dirt through your fingers, grass stains on your pants and
leaving muddy footprints at the door;
I want you to understand our planet, gain knowledge through
experience and be brave enough to explore.

This is how I want you to grow up.
Having good role models, with various backgrounds and from all
walks of life;
Teaching you kindness, teaching you resilience, teaching you
empathy;
I want you to learn important lessons, to be open minded and to
appreciate your elders.

This is how I want you to grow up.
Wearing blue pants, playing with trucks and going out on the
farm with your dad;
Understanding you are powerful, knowing there are no limits and
that you do not need to fit into any box;
I want you to learn that a colour does not define you, that you
seek out the path that makes you happy, that women can do
anything.

This is how I want you to grow up.
Playing with second-hand toys, wearing op-shop clothes and odd
socks;
Finding happiness in not what you wear but who you are,
supporting others and helping the environment;
I want you to learn to appreciate things, to be compassionate and
comfortable in your own skin.

This is how I want you to grow up.
With a hands-on father, one who teaches you things and tucks
you in at night;
Understanding that there are good men, safe men and loving men;
I want you to appreciate his love, his affection and his kindness.

This is how I want you to grow up.
Watching me speak, watching me listen and watching me do;
Understanding I'm always there, knowing I want the best for you,
keeping me accountable;
I want you to witness my wins, learn from my mistakes and know
that I'm doing my best.

This is how I want you to grow up.

She wins

I hope she never loses her zest for life. That she continues to jump in muddy puddles when she no longer watches Peppa Pig, and runs with her arms above her head and her joy above her pride when she's probably "old enough to know better".

I hope she will know that she's never too old, or too proud, or too big.

I hope she never stops enjoying the small things when she understands the big. That she will continue to find contentment in the sound of the rain on the roof, the way the leaves blow in the wind, and the colour the sky turns before and after a storm.

I hope she will know to try and see the beauty in the simple when everything can seem so complex.

I hope her unconditional and courageous love never fades. That she will know how much she deserves. That she is brave enough to find it and brave enough to keep it. But only if it deserves to be kept. That she continues to pour her heart into others that fill her own without fear that it may be broken.

I hope she will know that life's too short not to take the risk, and too long not to be happy.

I hope she never loses her haste to forgive, and that she knows forgiveness of herself is perhaps the most important. That she will know the power of moving forward rather than moving nowhere. That she will see that pride can always take the backseat without effecting her journey.

I hope she will know to always try to see the good, in others and herself. Because it is always there, somewhere.

I hope that she never stops letting her tears fall easily, or her smiles come naturally, her objection speak freely. That her feelings continue to be expressed as she feels them and her views continue to be known as she forms them.

I hope she will know that her strength is in being both strong and weak, and feeling the weak is what can make her the strongest.

I hope that as time passes and the world around her gets smaller, she continues to live, laugh and love large, like she is now.
Freely and with conviction.
Honestly and carefree.
Because that is the winning recipe.
And she deserves to win.

I hope.
She may.
But I need to lead by example first.

Dear Sleep-Deprived Toddler Mother,

I know you didn't think it would still be going on now, but it is.
They say it's a newborn thing,
They will start sleeping through,
You will sleep again soon.
But "they" are not always right, are they?

For some of us, they still wake numerous times, some nights.
They are still in your bed, some nights.
They still sleep on you in the old feeding chair, some nights.
You still sleep beside the cot with your arms through the bars,
some nights.
It is just as it was in the newborn days, when that was "expected".
Now it's only expected by you, as you wonder each night how
much sleep you may or may not get.

They are not only running laps around you during the day, but
also at night. And you feel like you are running laps too.
From the bed, to them;
From them, to beside the cot;
And back to bed, if you're lucky.
It's not a race, for there is no end in sight at the moment. You just
keep running in circles together in the dark hours.

It's not for want of trying either.

Both of you are trying, every time you meet in the early hours.

You want sleep.

You need sleep.

You need help.

So, you look into sleep plans, routine and read, you do LOTS of reading.

You listen and live by trial and error. However, trial becomes lesser as there becomes more "error". Well, that's what it feels like when you divert away from the "plan" for the trial that night and welcome the "rods".

You shouldn't feel like you have failed, but you do.

They are trying in their own way too.

By calling for you, by reaching for you through the bars, by sitting up waiting to be picked up by the arms that have always been there to help them.

They want sleep too.

They need sleep too.

But they need help too and this is their way of asking for it.

I'm not here to tell you anything you don't already know, but do know that you're not the only one that still meets your not-so-little one in the darkness, months after the newborn phase.

I've been there too.

There are lots of us.

Because despite what they say, and despite all efforts on both parts, some toddlers and some mothers just don't sleep through,

Yet.

For now

Mama,

I see you,
Waking up when you're not ready, tending to them with the energy you don't have, wondering what else you could do differently, reading everything, trialling anything, but nothing. Nothing works, nothing feels easy, nothing seems fair.

I see you,
Starting each day with an empty tank, digging into your reserves, forever hoping tonight will be different, comparing.
Comparing yourself, comparing them, comparing everything to anything.

I see you,
Catnapping with your eyes open, operating with your eyes closed, wanting to do everything, but struggling.
Struggling to do anything, struggling to feel "normal", struggling to be the mum you know you can be.

I see you,
Initially wanting to vocalise your struggles, to feel validated and not alone, but eventually not saying anything, just coping.
Coping internally, coping silently, coping this way because no

sleep has become your normal.

I see you,
Doing your best in the circumstances, surviving the conditions,
always wondering.
Wondering how much more you can take, wondering what will
make the difference, wondering when this too shall pass.

I see you,
Exhausted Mama whose toddler is still not sleeping through.
I've been there, I get it.
But please know that it does pass,
You do sleep again,
You will get through it.

I can see this now,
Because finally I'm on the other side, out of the blur, sleeping
again, for now.
For now, I can think straight, for now I can operate properly, for
now I'm able to be the mum I want to be.
I cannot predict how long it will last, but for now is enough.

Your for now will come, Mama,
And when it does, sometimes you will find yourself next to them
after they have fallen into a deep sleep that will remain unbroken,
ironically missing some of those broken moments you desperately
wished away before.

I want you to see this too.

Dear Pregnant-with-a-Toddler Mother,

"Is it bed time yet?"

I find myself asking this more than ever during my second pregnancy.
"Please come home soon".
I find myself saying this more than ever too.

It doesn't mean that I don't appreciate the time with my toddler or that I'm not coping, it just means that pregnancy with a toddler can be hard work, really hard work.

I haven't had a bad pregnancy by any means, but even so, some days dealing with the big emotions of a little person, while hormones serve you (an ever-expanding bigger person) with your own big emotions, can seem like the perfect storm.

You want to start out every day well, and you try to, but it can be something as simple as a wrong-coloured cup, or a missing teddy, or a something they don't even know is wrong, to steer the ship into unsettled waters.

Some days, particularly in the second trimester, you have enough energy to navigate through it. To source the right-coloured cup, to find the teddy or to work out what is wrong. Crisis averted and back into calm oceans you go.
Relief.

Other days, your hormones are sharp, your energy is edgy and your patience is blunt. You can wake up feeling sick, or tired, or both.

Something as simple as an unmade bed, a missing sock or an overcooked cake can steer the ship into what only can be described as internal torrential conditions.

It can feel like big emotions crashing into you, while you try your best to harbour your own on the inside in the only room you have left.

And the room inside gets smaller and smaller, as the little one inside you gets bigger and bigger.

With everything you have, you try to remain calm with patience that is worn, to remain energetic with the energy that is depleted and to be the thriving mum, when all you can muster is surviving. The energy harbouring these feelings is big too. It's no wonder you can't wait for your own bedtime.

"Your home", relief.

Their bedtime, relief.

Your bedtime, relief.

I know that being a mother is a privilege.

I know that being pregnant is a privilege.

I am beyond grateful for both and do not take either for granted.

It's just that some days are like this right now,

Because pregnancy with a toddler can be hard work.

And I'm allowed to say that without a disclaimer,

And so are you.

Dearest child,

The gradual outgrow

Your legs wrap around me, but not like they used to.
They are not as light now and they no longer tuck neatly under
my arms and chest.
Your feet either dangle below my waistline or nearly meet each
other on my opposite hip.

Your head burrows into my neck, but not like it used to.
There is not as much room now and it's only every now and then
that you try.
Your head is bigger than before and increasingly favours the spacious
underlay of your cot over the narrowing hollows of my neck.

Your hands clasp to me, but not like they used to.
They take hold less frequently now, and often try for the lining of
my clothing rather than the edges of my skin.
Your hands are more independent than before and you
increasingly use them to communicate your feelings rather than to
latch onto mine.

Your voice pines for me, but not like it used to.
Your cries are less distressed now and signal far more than a basic
need that I know I can meet.
Your tears flow heavier than before, and I am no longer the only
one you want to wipe them away.

Your eyes follow me, but not like they used to.
They are more easily distracted by their surroundings now, and
seek out anything that fills them with wonder.
Your line of vision is wider than before, and indicates your
realisation that there is more to life than just me.

You still need me, but not like you used to.
Every part of you is growing, evolving and changing, like it always
has.
You are slowly moving away from me, into yourself and into the
world, like you must.

But know that while you may outgrow me,
I will continue to remain here for you, arms ready to outstretch,
Waiting for the moment that you still need your mum.

Reunited

Sometimes I can't wait to hand you over, just for a moment, so I can mop the floor, hang the washing out and have a cup of tea.

Sometimes you don't want to go into the arms of another, but I need it, just for a moment, so that I can have my independence, you can learn to trust and someone else can benefit from your cuddles.

Sometimes you need to be taken out of view, just for a moment, so that you can be distracted, so that I can stop feeling worried by the cries, so that someone else can carry the load for a bit.

In those sometimes moments, I think we all win.
It doesn't happen a lot but it is good practise.
You socialise.
I feel independent.
Someone else gets more of you.

Always when you come back, I can't wait to hold you again, for a long while, so I can hear about your little trip, kiss you on the cheek and feel the warmth of our special connection.

Always you want to come back into my arms, for a long while, so that you know I am there, so that you remember I will always come back, so that you know I haven't forgotten about you.

Always you want my smile to be your view when we meet again, for a long while, so you know that I am proud of you for being brave, so you know I am happy to see you, so you know I missed you.

In those always moments, you and I win.
It happens without fail every time we are reunited after a break, no matter how long or short.
You remember,
I remember,
We are home.

If only you knew

If only you knew,
Not always giving you what you want is to help you, not hurt you.
The lollies you reach for at breakfast, the scissors you want to play with and the thistles you long to pick like flowers.
I stop you because I'm protecting you.
The worry for you is relentless, even if you think I'm stealing your happiness.
One day I hope you understand,
One day I hope you know,
But for now, please be patient.

If only you knew,
Not being able to console you sometimes is as hard on me as it is on you.
Leaving you for a moment, waiting for you to come back, watching you get upset.
I do this because I've tried everything.
The tears are sometimes shared between us, even if you don't see mine.
One day I hope you understand,
One day I hope you know,
But for now, please trust me.

If only you knew,
Being apart is about supporting each other, not caring less.
Sharing you with others, giving me time alone, allowing us to ease
into the inevitable separation.
I do this because we both need it.
It's about us growing together, even if it doesn't seem like it.
One day I hope you understand,
One day I hope you know,
But for now, please allow it.

If only you knew,
Me getting frustrated is more about me than you.
The raised voice, the mutters, the rolling eyes.
I do this when I lose control of my feelings.
I don't mean to direct my frustration at you, even when I do.
One day I hope you understand,
One day I hope you know,
But for now, please forgive me.

If only you knew,
The days I can't give you everything are those I struggle with
most.
The missed playgroup, the convenient meals, the screen babysitter.
I do this because life has other demands.
I always try to do better tomorrow, even if I can't.
One day I hope you understand,
One day I hope you know,
But for now, please go easy.

If only you knew,
Every day you open my heart and fill it simultaneously,
With unconditional love, daily learnings, everything I am to you.
You do this because I'm your mum.
You are remarkable, even if you don't know it yet.
One day you will understand,
One day you will know,
Because I'll make sure you do.

Two years of you

You met me first
You were so small
You made me Mum
You changed it all

The way I think
The way I act
The way I feel
The way I nap

The shows I watch
The songs I sing
The decor I buy
The snacks I bring

The things I want
The things I need
The things I value
The things I read

The fatigue I feel
The slow I go
The mess I keep
The love I know

The reasons I do
The reasons I don't
The reasons I sink
The reasons I float

The fears I have
The worry I bear
The chaos I live
The things I wear

You flipped my world
You opened my heart
You came here first
You were the start

You have since grown
You are now two
You made time fly
I'm shocked, it's true

Two years of you
Two years of us
Two years to remember
So celebrate we must!

CHAPTER SIX

DEAR HEARTBROKEN MOTHER

It may not be your time now, tomorrow, next month or next year, but I hold hope that someday a rainbow will follow your storm.

Losing you

Ashamed,
Helpless,
Broken,
This is how I felt.

Frustration,
Guilt,
Pain,
This is what I lived.

Cried,
Cursed,
Hid,
This is how I reacted.

Why me?
Why now?
Why at all?
This is what I asked.

I have failed,
I should have done it differently,
I am to blame,
This is what I convinced myself.

It wasn't meant to be,
It's not your fault,
At least it happened early,
This is what everyone said.

I was pregnant with number two,
I got to eight weeks,
There was no heartbeat.
This is what happened.

Seeing the light

When you are in the thick of trauma, time can feel slow, drawn out and hard to quantify. However, as time passes, as it always does, it can begin to feel fast, short-lived and difficult to recollect. It has the ability of making a dark picture more colourful, a difficult experience a learning, a negative a positive.
Not always, but sometimes.
Thankfully, I am an example of the sometimes.

Some time ago, I was living in the darkness of my miscarriage. Although I tried, I couldn't see the colour in much at all. As I sat once again in the chair at Medlab having my bloods taken, everything felt cold. The chair, the needle, the air.
The mood felt colourless and cold in almost every way. My smiles were forced and my pleasant conversations a mask for the hurt I was truly feeling.

Months later, I felt differently about my experience with loss. I was more learned, positive, and I lived in the excitement of my new pregnancy. While the colour remained a darker shade of brightness than it would have been had I not miscarried earlier, it still shone bright. I felt grateful and had restored the faith in my body.

I was not having to sit in the leather chair any longer, but I could then see the warm parts from the testing chapter. The warmth from the nurse's smile, from my toddler's bottom on my lap and from the sun shining through the window onto my back. My smiles became natural and my conversations were a true reflection of my positive outlook at the time.

I could see the light again, and time had helped.

My story is an example of the rainbow after the storm, the light after the darkness, the warmth after the cold.

It can happen.

It does, for many.

But I'm one of the lucky ones. Sadly, not everyone will share this story, and my heart breaks for those who still see only the dark shades despite significant lengths of time passing.

I'm sorry, so sorry.

All I can hope is that over time the shades lighten and you too will one day look back at the darkness with colour.

I hold hope for you, and I hope that you still hold hope for the light to shine, in your own time and in your own way.

The rainbow

Worry,
Before any test;
Before any scan;
Before you hear a heartbeat;
Before you sense any movement;
Before you feel any growth from within.

You hope for the best and try to remain optimistic, but until you get there, until you can see it and believe it, you are worried about what may not be.

And when you get there, you feel relief.

Relief,
When you see the two lines;
When you see movement on the screen;
When you hear a heartbeat;
When you sense a flutter;
When you feel a kick.

And when you get there, you feel excitement.

Excitement,
When you know that you can get pregnant again;

When you know they are viable;
When you know they are healthy;
When you know they are developing;
When you know things are as they should be.

This is what pregnancy after miscarriage can feel like.
Worry, relief, excitement.
On repeat and in that order.

In this season, the emotions of relief and excitement don't always last long because the cycle keeps turning, but each breeds a deep gratitude for what you have, what could be, and what others may not be so lucky to experience.
They give you the reassurance, confidence and strength that you need to quash the worrisome feelings that continuously meddle, even just for a moment. And that's enough.

It's a different kind of pregnancy, this sort.
It's not any less amazing, less special or less beautiful, but your past experience demands a self-protection of sorts, a coat of armour, a life jacket if you will.
And you are more than happy to wear it, for that extra weight and hassle you carry throughout is worth every ounce of the relief, excitement and gratitude that you know will follow when you can take off the life jacket and feel their skin on yours for the very first time.

I can still remember

I can still remember the day my miscarriage started.
I can still remember the exact date, the time, the weather.

I can still remember how I felt when I miscarried.
I can still remember the emotion, the questions, the emptiness.

I can still remember how others responded to my miscarriage.
I can still remember their words, their expressions, their impact.

I can still remember what I did when I miscarried.
I can still remember the hiding, the breaking, the optimistic research.

I can still remember what I told myself when I miscarried.
I can still remember the self-blame, the self-shaming, the self-loathing.

I can still remember the months following my miscarriage.
I can still remember the delays, the waiting rooms, the specialists.

I can still remember these things because they were a difficult part of my story.

I will always remember this chapter.
The pain, the heartache, the rawness of it all.

How could I forget?
I often want to,
But I don't, I can't, I won't.

It is deserving of a place in my story, just as every exciting or
enjoyable part is.

And while some choose not to share, a decision I completely
respect, it's a chapter that we should be encouraged to share, not
sweep under the carpet and dismiss.

Because every chapter, no matter how good, bad or indifferent, is
part of the story,
My story, your story, their story.

And it is a part of the story which, if you choose to share, may
help someone else reading it or hearing it feel a little less alone.

CHAPTER SEVEN

DEAR PENDING MOTHER OF TWO

The best is yet to come, even if you can't quite believe it yet.

We choose family

We are not your perfect family.
We go to the beach for the weekend and spend too much time
inside our room watching television.
We choose to eat ice creams for lunch over pre-made ham and
lettuce sandwiches.
We don't take enough nappies and forget sunblock.

But this is us.
This is how we family a lot of the time.
Forgetfully, imperfectly.
And to us, that's perfectly normal.
This is our normal.

One's exhausted from growing rapidly, one's exhausted from being
pregnant, one's exhausted from working hard, and one's exhausted
from being busy every moment of every day while awake.
We are exhausted.

One isn't being walked on the beach as recommended by health
professionals, one's trying to stay awake with coffee, one's
watching sport, and one's on yet another bottle of milk to give us
a few rare minutes of peace.
We are surviving.

One doesn't know what the world is about to offer, one doesn't know how she's about to juggle it all, one doesn't know whether he's about to be completely outnumbered, and one doesn't know what is about to turn her whole world upside down.
We are blind.

One's about to be a younger sibling, one's about to become a mum of two, one's about to work even harder, and one's about to have to learn to share.
We are changing.

There are no two ways about it.
Growing a family can be exhausting, raising a family can be exhausting, and being part of a family can be exhausting.
And it's not just because of the physical implications, but the emotional too.
It demands a lot, from everyone, every day.

Yet we choose to do it all over again.
We choose to grow.
We choose to be a bigger number, need a bigger car and have a bigger heart.
We choose imperfect.

Because at the end of the day, for us, exhaustion, uncertainty, change and imperfect is what gives us perfect.
It gives us family.

The beautiful predicament

Soon it will be different.
I may not be able to comfort her in the way I have come to know.
Straight away, smiling with her embrace, being her everything
right then, right now.
I'll try, but I can't be sure.
I'll always comfort her and be there for her even when she doesn't
think she needs me, but change is brewing.
I know it is.
Of course it is.
I'm going from one to two after all.

As I approach the final stretch of my pregnancy, this is perhaps my
biggest worry.
It's not about the birth, or the feeding or the postpartum changes
like it was the first time around.
It's about what will change for us, for our connection, for how we
operate.

At the moment, I can be there right away, I can answer to her
there and then, and all my energy is hers to have.
But soon things will look different.

It may look like me getting to her, but late.
It may look like me trying to comfort her, but after depleted

energy has stolen my smile.

It may look like our one-on-one time is instead having to be two-on-one.

It may look like a lot of things, which are different to our current.

It also may look like nothing I am describing because it's different to what I imagine.

I just don't know what different will be the new normal.

What I do know is that I am elated to be growing our family and to meet the new addition.

But the predicament still exists.

I still only have two hands and one heart.

They will soon need to be shared.

I want to be there for my first little in the same way I have been,

But I also want to be there for my second little in the same way at the same time.

Is this possible?

Maybe not.

Am I being greedy?

Maybe I am.

Is this a normal feeling?

Maybe, I have no clue.

But what a beautiful predicament to be in,

And how lucky I am to have this be my biggest problem.

Thanks to her

I should be resting. I am trying to rest. But my mind doesn't ever really switch off.

It is all over the show with what is about to come. It is full to the brim with questions, worry, excitement, anticipation, wonder, gratitude, tiredness, and Google search results.

The waiting and the unknowns, they all take their toll.
I had this the first time round, but not like this.

I had no idea what to expect with any aspect of pregnancy, birth or motherhood back then. And I'm not talking about all the things we read in textbooks. I'm talking about the things we learn through experience.

I didn't know how incredible the female body is or how much pressure it is placed under during pregnancy.

I didn't know how much birth would empower me, or turn my mind to what could go wrong.

I didn't know how much motherhood would shape me, or challenge every part of me.

I didn't know how precious of a gift it is to experience the entire journey, or what it is to experience loss.

And I didn't quite understand what is at stake throughout it all, a child who steals your heart.

Now I do, and it's a lot to comprehend.

Knowledge is power, but I feel powerless in the midst of my mind right now. It's constantly torn, a battleground of knowledge and experience.

I just want to cherish the last few moments of my pregnancy, because I know it's sacred.
But I also just want to get to the birth now and know that everything is ok.

I just want to cherish the time with my eldest, because I know everything will be different soon.
But I also just want to have my heart stolen again and start this new chapter.

My mind won't surrender. Not this time. And there is a very good reason for that.

It's all thanks to the girl who stole my heart first.

Thanks to her, I worry so much more, I overthink so much more and I feel so much more.

Thanks to her, I see so much more, I embrace so much more and I cherish so much more.

Thanks to her, I know so much more, I question so much more and I love so much harder.

Thanks to her, I know it's all worth it,
And that's everything worth battling over.

A new new

Dear Pending Mother of Two,

You wonder how can you do this with more.
It's hard enough with one.
How can I add to the hard?
Where's the room?
How will I cope?
I know you do, because I've been there.
And this is what I want to tell you.

You will get thrown into the deep end of postpartum again.
There's such a newness of everything, even though you've been there before.
A new little person to get to know.
A new body to learn to love.
A new life as a family of four to adjust to.

It's a new new.
And walking this territory can all feel a little overwhelming at times.
A little hard.
A little like you have no idea what you are doing.
And there will be tears, and cold tea, and forgotten dates.
And that's normal.

Because you have never done this sort of new before.
Remember that, ok?

But that's only part of it.
There is so much more to this new new.

There's the additional love that fills you, your home, your life and all those empty spaces you didn't even know were there.

There's a growing bond between two of your favourite people that will leave you feeling completely and utterly speechless, because no words can possibly describe how amazing it is, or how amazing they are.

There's even more for you and your husband to spend your never-enough time talking, smiling and scrolling over. You may feel further apart, but you are brought closer than ever. Truly.

There's the realisation that fully leaning into what works for you as a mother is the only thing worth spending your now halved energy on.
And it's freeing.

There's the nights and days that are filled with the best kind of chaos. The chaos that always sees through the tired and remembers only the beauty. Because it is beautiful, so beautiful.

And there's the old new that helps you with the new new. And eventually it's not so new anymore. It's your new normal. And you will wonder what you did with the time you had with one.
But you wouldn't go back.

Not a chance.

So pending mother of two, please don't worry.
The best is waiting for you.
Truly.
Remember that, ok?

Dearest child,

Please

For a while longer,
Let me hold you in my arms on your own,
Let me wipe away your tears with my hands that are only yours,
Let me soak in all of you every moment with every part of me.
Please let me,
Please,
We don't have much time.

For a while longer,
Let me hold your hand when we walk with ease,
Let me catch all of your smiles without interruption,
Let me not take any of you for granted.
Please let me,
Please,
We don't have much time.

For a while longer,
Let me be the one to console you when you cry for me,
Let me be the one to pick you up when you tug at me,
Let me be the one to come to you without delay.
Please let me,
Please,
We don't have much time.

Forever,
You will be my eldest child,
You will be the one who made me Mama,
You will be the one who first extended my heart.
Please know this,
Please,
Nothing will change that.

Forever,
I will be there for you,
I will cherish you,
I will love you,
Please know this,
Please,
Nothing will change that.

But soon,
There will be two of you,
There will still be one of me,
Things will be different.

So for a while longer,
Please let me,
Please,
Give every part of me to only you,
Soak up every part of you with only me,
Enjoy every moment of it being only us.
Please let me,
Please,
We don't have much time.

It's not long now

Little one, it's not long now.
I know I haven't been resting enough, or taking long baths whenever I feel the need, or whispering to you as much as I would like.
You must wonder if I care sometimes.
I do, I absolutely do.
It's just that I have been caught up chasing your older sister around, spending late nights trying to settle her and answering her with my whispers.
She needs me in a different way, a way you will need me one day too.

Little one, it's not long now.
I know I don't take too many bump photos, have your nursery completely set up or have my hospital bag packed just yet.
You must wonder if I have forgotten about you sometimes.
I haven't, I absolutely have not.
It's just that I'm more experienced now. I still look at you in the mirror every day and smile. My hospital bag and your nursery will be ready in time, I promise.

Little one, it's not long now.
I know I don't always eat the most nourishing of foods, drink enough water or exercise as much as recommended.

You must wonder if I want to give you the best sometimes.

I do, I absolutely do.

It's just that my body and mind are more tired this time, as they're being pulled between you and your sister, but I am trying to do my best for you every single day. Please know I'm trying my best.

Little one, it's not long now.

I know I can be riddled with mixed emotions some days, and there can be no predicting the conditions. I know you feel this too.

You must wonder if I'm ok sometimes.

I am. I absolutely am.

It's just that my body is going through a lot right now and my mind sometimes doesn't understand this. It's not your fault, none of it. OK?

Little one, it's not long now.

I know this hasn't always been the easiest ride for us.

You must wonder a lot.

But please don't.

To me, you are perfect and part of my everything already.

I cannot wait to meet you soon, little one.

It's not long now.

CHAPTER EIGHT

DEAR NEW MOTHER OF TWO

You are doubling the chaos, but also the love.

Times two

Back to square one, but with two.

You have more experience this time, but there's still a newness as you adjust to life as a fresh family of four.
And honestly speaking, there are some crucial differences within this transition.

Cooking standards stoop even lower than you thought possible, remembering frozen meals only last so long.

There's no sleep when the baby sleeps, unless both littles sleep at the same time. This appears to be a rarity.

There's less time to sit and gaze at the newborn, or play with the toddler, unless one of them is napping and the other plays ball for a while allowing it.

There's more guilt as you're spread thinner than before. While spending time feeding the newborn, you feel like you're failing in your duties to the eldest. While reading to the toddler, you feel like you're neglecting crucial bonding responsibilities to your newborn.

There's more surviving as you do more with the same number of hands you've always had. The rods are well and truly welcomed and the cares for the "shoulds" are left standing outside in the cold, blatantly ignored as they continue to knock on the door.

There's no wiggle room for any "I" in team. There shouldn't be, no matter how many children you have together, but you realise this the more you have. After work, they tag in with both littles while you tag out for something as little (but big) as a shower. They then tend to one, while you tend to the other. This carries on into the dark hours, but no one tends to your relationship.

Finding time for yourself is even harder. It takes real discipline that you rarely have the energy for. And too often after the fact, or meltdown, or moment of madness, you realise you should've followed your own rules. You should've had the coffee instead of vacuuming after all.

But honestly, you do get through the days and nights, the guilt, the exhaustion, the tagging in and out, the constant selflessness, because of them, because of everything they are to you, because of everything you are to them.

And in all honesty, there's a reason you decide to have more children,
And that reason isn't because it's not hard,
But because it's worth it,
Honestly.

Day in the life

It was 4am.
I fed the baby, changed him, then spent an hour resettling him.
I got back to bed at 5.30am.
Getting back to sleep didn't happen.
My husband was getting ready for work.
My toddler woke.
I fed her breakfast, changed her, and spent half an hour settling a tantrum.
Then I unloaded the dishwasher, made the beds and put a load of washing on.
I started reading her a book.
The baby woke.
I stopped reading, had to diffuse a tantrum while feeding the baby and forgot about eating my breakfast.
I fed him for nearly an hour.
I parented my toddler from afar while her emotions crashed into me.
I felt the brunt of them, but managed to regulate mine. Somehow.
My baby fell asleep feeding, so I tried to put him in his cot.
My toddler followed me.
I closed the door, leaving her on the other side.
She made her presence known anyway.
That woke him.
We repeated the cycle in the baby's bedroom.

"We" managed to get him down this time.

I carried my toddler to the living room, begging her to stay quiet.

I offered her morning tea.

She didn't like what I made.

I read her three books.

She finally fell asleep.

It was noon.

I hung out the washing, got meat out for dinner, called my husband about something which seemed important.

And the baby woke.

And he was fussy.

So we paced the hallway. Over and over.

Then my toddler woke.

I tended to them both. Her at my knees demanding and him at my hip crying.

I fed them both, somehow.

I then took them outside.

We sat under a tree.

We watched the leaves.

I explained the colours.

This is all that worked.

And I'd tried everything.

My husband came home.

Somehow it was 5pm.

How was it that late?

I cooked dinner.

He bathed them.

We ate dinner.

We consumed tears.

The baby fell asleep.

My husband attempted the toddler's bedtime.

I dealt with the mess of the day.
The baby woke again.
It was 9pm.
I fed and resettled him.
Finally they were both asleep.
It was 10.30pm.
I still hadn't showered.
Or hung the washing out.
Or eaten enough.
Or lots of things actually.
But I made it.
For the next few hours at least.
Maybe until tomorrow.
And tomorrow I'll try again.
Because that's what mothers do.

Laced with magic

The days right now consist of a lot of the mundane.

Changing nappies, wiping faces, finding breast pads, routine swaddling, cleaning sheets, soaking stains, hanging washing, using washing before it's put away, finding sippy cups, sterilising breast pumps, feeding snacks, assembling something edible for dinner, scrubbing elephant-shaped plates, bathing littles, bathing them again, picking up toys, picking up clothes, picking up crusts, picking up everything for everyone.

But the mundane is laced with moments of magic.

The little loves that come when you're feeling down, the "luff you Mum" when you least expect, the infectious smiles that make up for everything, the late-night snuggles that calm you as much as them, the sibling hand-holds that make your heart melt, the little noises that echo like a lullaby from the bassinet, the new words that always come too early, the early-morning bed parties that warm your insides as much as the sheets on which you lay, the little hands that reach for your chin while you feed them, the way they look at you for the longest time without needing a reason, the pleasure they get from something as simple as splashing bathwater.

Some days it can be hard to see the magic in the mundane.
Exhaustion, overwhelm and hormones can rid you of that.
But the thing about motherhood is that even if the lace is invisible some days, it's there every day, holding the moments of mundane, madness and mess together.
And when you see it, no matter for how long or how often, it's what holds you together too.

Caught up

I'm caught up in them.

You'll find me sitting up in bed under dim lighting and sprawled sheets at night, feeding him every few hours.

I'll be reading to her while tending to him in the same position on the green couch in the living room much of the day.

I'll be changing nappies, washing little clothes and wiping pencil marks off walls during the moments that allow me my own hands.

I'm caught up in them.

I'll watch him longer than I need to, because the way he curls up into me, smiles with his eyes closed and makes little sleeping noises is infectious.

I'll play with her past her normal bedtime, because the time we have on our own now is lesser, I want to enjoy her too and these are our little moments to cherish.

I'll be thinking about them, scrolling through photos and talking about them like we haven't been together for days whenever we're not together for the shortest time.

I'm caught up in them.

I'll leave my coffee and toast to go cold because he needs a nappy change, because she needs a kiss better, or if all I need is a moment wrapped up in everything they are.

I'll forget to use conditioner, to put the bins out or about the washing on the line, because I'm too busy thinking about them during the moments that I have my own mind.

I'll take longer to finish what I start, to tick things off the list or to do anything needing to be done, because they come first right now but won't always need to.

I'm caught up in them.

The way he cries for me and then settles when we touch, the way she says "Mum and Dad" when she first wakes up, the way they both take from me every moment of every day but give me even more, is my daily fuel.

This is why I'm caught.
And this why I'll be caught up in them for as long as they will let me be.

I'm caught up in them.

Go figure

As a mother the second time around, I do things differently.

The way I mother is different.

The way I am is different.

I'm so much more relaxed and carefree.

And it has been freeing.

But the way I mothered the first time round was what felt right at the time.

So, it was right at the time.

And that mother was important.

She paved the way for the mother I am now.

I needed to be her, to get to where I am now, not be told I needed to get to where I am now when I was her.

And that's important too.

Because we get there.

But we need to get there in our own time and in our own way.

We just need to figure it out for ourselves.

Dearest child,

Little adjustments

I'd finally been able to hold him
The boy, second to steal my heart
But you were still there, in the forefront, right after
The night we'd been apart.

I was nervous about how it would go
I had no idea how you would cope
Being the eldest, the first, the one who made me Mama
All I could do was hope.

It had always been the two of us
A family of three had become our norm
A new addition, a fourth, my shared attention
Would you jump for joy or mourn?

Post birth I waited for the phone call
To hear that you were being brought in
So you could meet your new little brother, your sibling
And adjust to life with him.

I heard your feet down the hallway
They sped up as I called your name
"Mummy, Mummy, I'm coming", you yelled out loudly
Your excitement to see me untamed.

You burst through the door and hugged me
Peeping at the new boy in blue
Not yet understanding that he was ours to take home, your sibling
That he was our number two.

But as I cradled him, you stopped
Your little face shocked by the sight
Someone else so small in my arms, Mummy, really?
Did I get replaced overnight?

It took a few days for me to show you
That while it was no longer just us
You were not forgotten, or less important, not slightly
Your big sister role was a plus.

And I know some times have been hard
All the sharing and waiting was new
The undivided attention on you much less frequent
The times of you and I became few.

But before long, you came to realise
That this little baby is yours too
You love him just as much as we do, it's clear
You always want him in view.

So now I want you to know something
It's important to me that you do
You have handled it so well, my first baby, my girl
And for that I'm so proud of you.

Split by two

I miss you some days, and I often don't realise it until after 7.30pm, when the older of you two leaves time for just the two of us. Or when time allows us the quiet darkness, tired but uninterrupted.
It doesn't matter which.

It's often when we find each other fully for the first time since we wake.
That precious time when we can breathe each other in, and feel the depth of the connection you so often ask for during the day, which I cannot always give.

I see you on your bouncer and you smile at me, or reach out for me, or coo,
And I smile back, and coo.
Of course I do.
How could I not?
To me, you are perfect.

But as I reach for you, I'm so often pulled away by the needs of your sister instead.
She tells me she needs "that" book, or she's hurt her hand, or she doesn't like the dog inside.
And she can't wait.

No matter how hard I try.
She just doesn't quite understand that you need me too, just the same, just yet.

So I tend to her and leave you on the bouncer, or having tummy time, or lying in your cot.
You seem so understanding as your eyes follow me until I'm out of sight, waiting for me to come back so we can try again. So I can pick you up, and smile with you.
It's like you've become accustomed to it.
Like it's your normal.
And I feel so guilty.

But I want you to know.
You may not feel seen right now, but I see you.
I see everything about you.
I see you even when you're not seeing me see you.
When it's late and dark.
When you have fallen asleep next to me and I would rather fight sleep than end our time.

Because you've made me see,
It's about making the most of the small moments, the important moments, the moments I look forward to capturing and hate missing out on, no matter how fleeting.
It's quality over quantity that matters.
And you are of the finest quality.
Just as she is.

So I may be out of your sight sometimes.
But you're not out of mine.

I'm seeing you when it counts,
And I'm making it count.
Because you count,
Just as she does.

My learning

This is how some nights look. Me right there. Close to you.
The corners of books digging into my back, and my arm numb
underneath the growing weight of you.
But only when you let me,
Because now it's only then.

You used to always need me close at night, but I didn't always
oblige. Not in the very early days at least. And that pains me a
little now. I was finding my way as a new mum and getting lost in
all the books.

I would place you down in your cot and hope you would sleep.
And when you didn't, when you couldn't without my help, I'd so
often put my arms through the bars, touching you so I felt closer,
but being too far away for your liking. I fought the urge to pick
you up and cradle you, to let myself be your pillow.

And I thought that was the best thing for you. That if I didn't let
you learn on your own right away, that somehow you'd never be
able to do it on your own.

But how wrong I was.
How wrong the books were.
In my experience, anyway.

Before long I gave in. And it was easier on us both. You got there in your own time, and we got there in our own way, together.

But you're so much bigger now. Gone are the days of cots, swaddling and white noise drowning out every emotion. Gone too are the days of you always asking for me while you fall asleep. Here are the days of single beds, soft toys and cartoon duvets. Here too are the days of you needing me less.
And it's bittersweet.

So when you say "Mummy, hop in" and pat the space beside you, I always jump in without a hesitation or worry about what I may be undoing. Other than the things awaiting my attention outside of your single bed that is far too small for the two of us, nothing demands space in my mind.

I watch you fall asleep, desperately trying to make up for those early (some)times, where I read everything but you.
And often I fall asleep too, eventually waking to the sound of your brother who needs me, as you once did.

And I go to him. I hold him. I feed him to sleep. I follow his lead. And there are no bars between us, because I know that he too will get there, regardless of how much I oblige.

And it's thanks to you.
But I'm sorry you were my learning.
I'm learning too.

CHAPTER
NINE

DEAR STAY-AT-HOME MOTHER

You are doing work, arguably the most important work on the planet. Your worth is not defined by a pay check. If it were, no figure would ever come close to being enough.

It's different now

It's different now.
Success is quantified differently.
It's not about having a clear inbox, smashing budgets and being efficient within the workday.
It's about having a messy house, witnessing other's milestones and going at someone else's pace.

It's different now.
Failure is quantified differently.
It's not about missing deadlines, handling complaints or being demoted.
It's about not keeping someone safe, warm, fed and feeling loved.

It's different now.
Happiness is quantified differently.
It's not about having cool clothes, an expensive car and nice sunglasses.
It's about witnessing someone else smile at you, laugh with you and rely on you always.

It's different now.
Stress is quantified differently.
It's not about being late for a meeting, worrying about your career progression or whether you will meet your monthly target.

It's about hearing the cries all day, questioning whether you are doing enough and worrying about someone else's future.

It's different now.
Relaxation is quantified differently.
It's not about having the weekend off, having a holiday booked or taking all of your leave at once.
It's about getting five minutes alone, allowing yourself to remember who you are again and not feeling guilty about taking a break.

It's different now,
But it's the best sort of different.

Full-time job

Your office is your home.
You work there every day, but there are often no other staff
members to keep you company.

The staffroom is your bedroom.
You spend some time in there for meetings late at night and early
in the morning, but it is not ever for long enough.

The toilet and bathrooms are your daily break space.
You don't eat in either, but you try to get some alone time.

The lunch breaks take place whenever your little one naps.
You rarely take the opportunity to eat, instead attempting to get
all of your daily jobs done in those time slots.

The morning meeting takes place whenever you wake up.
You have no control over the time, but you have to be there.

There is no such thing as a 5pm knock-off.
You may get some help from then, but you are always on call.

You do not get a salary, nor can you charge out at an hourly rate.
Kisses and cuddles are the currency you receive, but that's more
than enough.

You cannot take sick days or long weekends alone.
You show up every day regardless, for you have the skills and trades that are relied upon.

You are not bound by the terms of any legal employment contract.
You are bound by love, the terms of which are to be figured out between you.

Being a mother is a full-time job.
It may be a different kind of job, but it's a job nonetheless.
In fact, it's one of the most important jobs you will ever have.

Just a Mum

You are not just a mum; you are someone's everything.
Their world.
Their protector.
Their comfort.
In you they see a level of safety no one else can provide.
In you they trust absolutely.
Just doesn't come into it.

You are not just a mum; you are the most important piece of someone's puzzle.
Their rock.
Their constant.
Their superhero.
In you they see everything you don't always see.
In you they believe absolutely.
Just doesn't come into it.

You are not just a mum; you are someone's jack of all trades.
Their cook.
Their teacher.
Their nurse.
In you, they see no limits to your devotion.
In you they rely absolutely.
Just doesn't come into it.

You are not just a mum; you are working in testing conditions.
No sleep.
No sick days.
No pay.
Through your sacrifices, they get everything.
Through you, they grow.
Just doesn't come into it.

You are not just a mum; you are raising the future.
The children.
The parents.
The grandparents.
Through your contributions, the world benefits.
Through you, it improves.
Just doesn't come into it.

You are not just a mum: you are so much more.
You are someone.
You are everyone.
You are everything to everyone.
"Just" just doesn't come into it.

Again

I'm holding my baby who just wants to be held, while watching my toddler about to do something she shouldn't, again.
I'm wearing my husband's hoody and eating leftovers from my child's plate, again.
I'm using a teaspoon because the forks are in the dishwasher unwashed, again.
I'm forgetting to breathe while I eat, again.
I haven't had nearly enough water today, again.
I still haven't had a shower today, again.
That reminds me, I still haven't rung the plumber, again.
So I must remember to put it on my to-do list, again.
My kitchen is messy, again.
No wait, everything is messy, again.
I need to wash the baby-bouncer cover, again.
Because that's been spewed on, again.
But I can't, because I've run out of washing powder, again.
And honestly I can't face getting the children back in the car to go to the shops, again.
Because that means I need to sort much of the above, which I don't have the energy for, again.
And I'm just so tired, again.
All this, and it's still only lunchtime, again.

And again, I'm sharing this part of motherhood.
And again, an unflattering photo documenting it will be saved.
Because again, this is what they see a lot of the time.
Doing things, again and again, for them, before me.
And sometimes not doing things again and again for me, after them.
That's what being a mother is.

And this is the part of motherhood that I will always be proud of.
And I want this to be documented, as much as the beautiful photos, and perfect moments, and memories of me investing in myself, which are rare but so important.

Because again and again, I show up for them first, and that shouldn't be the last thing I celebrate.
It shouldn't be left on my phone storage and deleted to make room for the perfect.
It shouldn't not be talked about or treated as just another mother complaining.
It deserves a place in a frame and an album.
It deserves a place in journals and books.

Because one day, it will serve as a reminder that I was their again, every day for years,
The hard but beautiful years.
And I'll never want to forget any of it.
I'll want to remember every single detail,
Again and again,
All over again.

Chapter Ten

Dear Working-from-Home Mother

Not all superheroes wear capes.
Some wear little humans while trying to meet deadlines.

Impossibly possible

Start, stop, forget what you started.
Start over, stop, forget what you started over.
Don't start, stop, forget what you didn't start.

Working from home while looking after young children.
It's one way to not finish anything you start and restart everything you haven't already finished.

You can feel like you are constantly chasing your tail. You go round and round in circles trying to get what you need to get done in a day, but as is the case with any circle, there is no start nor end.

Naptime is your saviour, if you are lucky enough to still have that, but that is only a small window of the day, and that window gets smaller and smaller as they grow bigger and bigger.
Regular naps.
Two naps.
One nap.
Half a nap.
No nap.

Night-time is often your only choice, if you are lucky enough to be able to keep your eyes open, but that is not sustainable every night, particularly if you are still on night shift.

Try to stay awake.
Try to sleep.
Sleep.
Awoken.
Try to stay awake.
Try to get back to sleep.

Sometimes you have no choice but to fill the gaps in between sleep, but that demands the most from you, physically and mentally. Your hands are already holding too much and your mind is full with guilt.
You shouldn't be working while they are there.
They need you more.
They have had too much screen time.
Other mums make it work.
(Insert further unhelpful guilt-driven thoughts here).

Sometimes you feel like you can't win, it's natural.
However, more often than not, you are winning because as a mum winning looks like getting something done rather than everything done.
It looks like celebrating the small victories, rather than celebrating only the big ones.
It looks like doing your best, not being the best.

The start, the stops, the interruptions are all part of working from home, but they are not all of it. There are the wins in between, even if they are hard to recognise.

Motherhood. It's just about seeing the "wins", rather than being blinded by the "losses". That's how I see it anyway.

Modern Mother

Mama,

There is only one of us.

We only have two hands, two feet and one brain.

We were created this way, but the context of motherhood used to be much different.

Mothers didn't work from home or work away. Day cares didn't exist and villages of family and friends helped raise a child every day.

Today there is still only one of us.

We have the same number of hands and feet, and one brain. Yet we are expected to carry a load far heavier than our physical and mental make-up allows.

We are expected to work, to be just as present with our children as if we didn't work, day cares have huge waiting lists, and daily villages of family and friends are harder to come by because everyone is either busy trying to meet these new expectations themselves or feeling like there is less of a need for them in someone's village due to the same.

Remember, it's not possible to do everything on your own.

Welcome the offerings of help and support when they come.

Farewell the feelings of pride and guilt when they surface.

Surrender to the impossible, always.

It's the only way to mother these days.

Sounding board

Mama,

Just in case no one asked you today,
How are you doing? How are you feeling? How are you actually?
How are you coping? Are you coping?
How have you been sleeping? Have you managed a shower? Did
you get through your emails?
What else do you need?
What was the highlight of your day? What really annoyed you?
What?
How?
Who?
It's not nothing. Can you tell me more? I want to hear all about it.
What was the lowest part of your day? Do you want to talk about
it? Do you not want to talk about it? We've all been there, so don't
be so hard on yourself, ok?

And Mama, just in case no one has told you today,
You and all you do is seen.
The cleaning, the cooking, the washing. The reading, the bathing,
the playing. The organising, the planning, the sorting. The
humouring, the consoling, the multitasking.
The projects you fit in between.
And don't worry, everything else isn't forgotten. There's too much

to list. The load is heavy, yet somehow you manage it. You are incredible. Thank you so much.

But it's ok if you are not managing it. Surviving is thriving in this season. Remember that, ok?

And you are doing such a good job. You are a great Mum. They are so lucky to have you.

And Mama, just in case you haven't told yourself today,
You look great as you are, however you are. With makeup or without makeup, filter or no filter, tucked or untucked.

No one cares about the mess in your home as much as you do. But if you want to clean it, clean it. You do you. Always do you. They want you, not someone else.

You are everything to them. You are the glue, the mortar, the heart, of both your home and your family. You may come unstuck, but they won't.

Follow your gut, your instinct, your dreams. You can still have dreams, you know. Dream big. You can do big things. Today, one day, when you're ready.

And Mama, just in case you need reminding,
Don't forget to make time for you, to spend money on you, and to be true to you.

Those things matter. You matter.

I hope you can see that.

CHAPTER ELEVEN

DEAR PERFECTLY IMPERFECT MOTHER

There is no such thing as perfect in motherhood.
If there were, there would be a manual.

Stress less

I am often the mum who stresses about cleaning my house before
visitors,
And trying to bake scones,
And doing my hair,
And my makeup,
And hiding the washing.

Yet when I visit others,
Who haven't got to the dishes,
And offer biscuits from the packet,
And confess they haven't had time to shower,
And move washing so we can fit on the couch,
I immediately feel at ease,
Like I'm not alone,
Like this is what I should embrace more and stress about less,
For myself and my visitors.

One day

One day I will look back on this time like a distant memory and when that day comes,

I won't say I wish that I spent more time cleaning, that I had time to iron my clothes, that the dishes got more of my attention.
I will say that living in mess was our reality but I'm glad I chose cuddles over cleaning, reading to them over ironing and playing with LEGO over doing dishes because it all went too quickly.

I won't say I wish that I got more sleep, that I didn't drink as much coffee, that I always knew what day of the week it was.
I will say that being tired was the normal, but I'd go back there in an instant for the beautiful raw connection in the early hours, the smiles when I least expected and the unconditional love I received, because I miss those moments.

I won't say I wish that I was stricter with their sleep schedules, that I stopped the bottle a bit earlier, that we had put them in bedrooms further away from ours.
I will say that some days were challenging, but that I'm glad I was always there for them when they needed me, that I made the "rods for my own back" and that they knew I was close because they don't need me as much as they once did anymore.

I won't say I wish that I had spent more time checking emails, that I'd answered more work calls, that they had slept for longer during the day so I could get more done.

I will say that the mum/work-life balance was a struggle, but I'm glad that I chose dancing to the Wiggles over checking emails, exchanging baby banter over work calls, late nights working over compromising our time during the day, because I have all the time to work on my own terms now.

I won't say I wish that I had more alone time to read my favourite books, that I could have gone to the toilet in peace, that the house was silent more often.

I will say that there was no peace and quiet but there is nothing quite like having tiny shadows, hearing the pitter-patter of little feet and living in a noisy home.

While the things I won't say sometimes seem important right now, in the small picture, they won't be later, in the big one.

I know I will say that too.

Bothered

Oh, how I'm grateful, so very grateful, to be a mother. Don't I know it. Don't I make sure I remind myself every waking minute. But yesterday was one of those "I can't be bothered" days. Controversial perhaps, but true.

I just felt like my breakfast, my coffee and dare I say it, having myself to myself for even just a moment.
I wanted not to be needed, or relied upon, or called on every minute.
I wanted to hear myself breathing, feel myself breathing, remember to breathe.
Some days it doesn't feel like there's the opportunity.

But oh, how I love them, so very much. Don't I know it. Don't I feel it with every inch of my being.
But some days I just want space.
To use both hands.
To finish what I start.
To do more than unload the dishwasher and call it a "win".

Yesterday was one of those days. I knew it as soon as I woke up. I could hear my daughter grizzling at 5am. She normally sleeps until 6am when her dad wakes.
Was there any point trying to resettle her?

Let's just get up now.

Oh, but I'm tired. I just want to lie here doing nothing. Resting my eyes without light, my ears without noise and my body without the pulls.
Is it too much to ask?
It all annoyed me. Normally it wouldn't.
What a dilemma. It wasn't, but it felt like one.

I tended to her, as I always do.
I made myself bother, as I always do.
Of course, I did. Because I love my children. I'd do anything for them. They are my everything.

But everything wasn't easy yesterday.
The rest of the day felt long and drawn out.
Surely it's 2pm already? Nope, it's 9.30am.
Please be bedtime already. Is 5pm too early for bed?

It bothered me that I felt this way too.
Oh, how I get bothered by feeling like this when these days happen.
Be grateful. You don't know how lucky you are. Enjoy every moment.
These thoughts are a constant bother.
Because I am those things. I do know. I do try.

Oh, how I'm grateful, so very grateful.
Oh, how I know how lucky I am, so very lucky.
Oh, how I love being a mum, so very much.

Don't I know it. Because I do. With every fibre.
I really do.

But some days I just can't be bothered being bothered all the time.
And yesterday was one of those days.

Today Mother

Yesterday I was the surviving mum.
I supervised screen time, we had takeaways for dinner and the washing was left on the clothes line.
I was the let-anything-go mum, the let's-write-off-today mum, the let's-try-that-tomorrow mum.
My fuse was short, my brain unmotivated and my body tired.
Wake time came too early and bedtime couldn't come early enough.
Nothing got achieved other than creating a huge pile of dishes, more washing and an overwhelming sense of guilt.

These days swallow me whole.
I tell myself that they will only remember these days.
The ones where I label myself the under-par mum, the mediocre mum, the lazy mum, because that's what I truly believe at the time.
I try to erase these days, like they are something to be embarrassed about.
"I'm a bad mum."
"Stop being so lazy."
"I can do better than this."
And I know I can,
Perhaps tomorrow but just not today.

So, I wait for tomorrow. Will it spit me out and let me try again?

It did.

Today I was the thriving mum.

We played outside most of the day, I managed to bake a cake and put away yesterday's washing.

I was the fun mum, the organised mum, the let's-get-it-done mum.

I had the patience of a saint, my mind was positive and I had energy to burn.

We woke up smiling and I forgot the time at night.

The day was filled with laughter and purpose and I was left full of all the good.

These days give me strength.

I tell myself that these are the days they deserve every day.

The ones where I feel like the good mum, the present mum, the made-to-do-this mum, because that's what I truly believe at the time.

I want to catch every moment of these days and hang them on the wall.

I am proud of them.

I remember what I'm capable of.

I don't want them to end.

But they do,

And there are no guarantees for the next.

Tomorrow I don't know what sort of mum I will be.

I want to be the today mum. I push so hard to be her always.

But that's not tenable. I can't be that mum every second of every minute of every hour of every day of every week of every month of every year.

That's what I need to tell myself and believe.

Because actually, that's the truth.

Motherland

Even if your children sleep through the night, you can still be tired.

Even if you have a break from them during the day, you can still feel completely touched out by bedtime.

Even if you practise all the calming techniques in the world, you can still explode sometimes.

Even if your to-do list is smaller than yesterday, it can still seem gigantic today.

And even if you do your best with all you have on the hard days, you will still tell yourself that your all wasn't enough.

There's a lot involved with being a mother.
It's more than mothering them. It's also mothering yourself.
It's bigger than all the "small", and the "big" is often so very small.
Allow yourself the grace to see that.

Motherhood's reason

It's because of the:
Hard days,
Sleepless nights,
Tantrums,
Constant mess,
That you learn to truly appreciate:
The good days,
The unbroken nights,
The cuddles,
The tidy home.

It's because of the:
Lukewarm coffee,
Leftovers of leftovers,
Constant noise,
Unfinished jobs,
That you learn to truly appreciate:
A hot coffee,
An entire meal,
Five minutes' peace,
Finishing what you start.

It's because of the:
"Natural" days,

Stained tops,
Worn-out shoes,
Chipped nails,
That you learn to truly appreciate:
Putting makeup on,
Wearing a freshly cleaned T-shirt,
Buying a new pair of shoes,
A manicure.

It's because of the:
Late nights cleaning,
Early morning organisation,
Stressful grocery shops,
Backseat grizzles,
That you learn to truly appreciate:
Early nights watching movies,
Sleep-ins past 7am,
Grocery shopping alone,
An empty car seat.

But...
It's also because of the:
Time apart,
Nights alone,
Growing independence,
New milestones,
That you learn to truly appreciate:
Your time together,
The nights of reliance,
The moments of dependence,
The speed of time.

Motherhood.
Without the hard parts, it would be difficult to truly appreciate
the amazing parts, and without a true appreciation of the amazing
parts, it would all be difficult to understand.
Everything has a reason.
This is motherhood's reason,
I think.

CHAPTER TWELVE

DEAR OVERWHELMED MOTHER

*Do you know why being everything to everyone
every moment of every day is so hard?
It's because it's impossible.
Take a deep breath and remember,
it's only possible to do your best.*

A rough day

Mama,

I know today has been rough. You have been putting out fires all day, while letting yourself become the ruins.

You are tired, so tired. That's nothing new, but today you feel particularly frayed at the edges. The layers of sleep are wearing thin right now and you feel like the thread of love is barely holding you together.

You feel a lot overwhelmed, not just a little. Individually the things are little, but collectively, everything has become a little big. What you would give to shorten the lists rather than add to the pages. But you just can't do it all.

You feel tapped out. You needed so many breaks that didn't come and you wanted to be held more than they needed you to hold them. It doesn't make sense really, but it never does. Motherhood is like that.

You love them more than anything in this world, but you just need five minutes without them within an inch of you. Even less, perhaps more. Just any time available to catch your breath and regroup. To remember who you are. To remember what you need.

To remember anything.

You pray that tonight will run smoothly and that tomorrow will be different. That by some miracle there will be less fighting and more surrendering. You need to surrender too. You know this, but it's easier said than done.

You will go to bed tonight and replay all of the rough. Then feel like you are failing it, or worse, that you are failing them. Then overthink the failings. Then not sleep.

But please don't, Mama.

Rest easy knowing that we all have rough days. That you did your best. That you are doing incredible things on what can feel like absolutely nothing.

Dream only of the lashings of beauty throughout the day, because they were there. They are always there somewhere, even if hidden in the shadows of the hard.

And finally, give yourself the chance for tomorrow to be better, because it can be. It often is. You just have to let go of today first.

Big and small

The big things to us are small to them.

The worry about how much screen time they have, any effect it's having on their development and the following guilt.

What seems big to us, is small to them.

They don't worry about the length of an episode, the best educational option or our guilt. They just enjoy saying "hi" to their favourite cartoon, seeing us relax into a smile as we get a moment and cuddling with us on the couch.

The stress over the way they should be sleeping, the "rods", the opinions we try to avoid.

What seems big to us, is small to them.

They don't worry about what age they slept through or what others think. They just want security in their darkest hours, to be listened to when they don't have the words, to dream easy.

The overthinking about whether we return to "work", stay at home or "work" from home.

What's big for us, is small to them.

They don't worry about how many days they're in care, if they're getting socialisation outside the home or if they've been left to play alone so you can send an email. They just want to be happy, to see you happy, to feel loved.

And the small things to us are big to them.

The way we look at them, cuddle them and say things.

What seems small to us, is big to them.

We don't always notice every smile we return, whether our hands are warm when we hold theirs or how funny we sound saying "Moo". But they do. These little things are their everything.

The way we get down to their level and talk with them, cut off their crusts and spend time listening to their long-winded stories.

What seems small to us, is big to them.

We sometimes don't see the magic of meeting them where they are, making it a little easier for them, hearing them for them. But they do. These are smile makers and cry breakers.

The time taken to read an extra story, to cuddle them a little longer, to kiss them goodnight.

What seems small to us, is big to them.

We sometimes lose sight of how much the intangible and inexpensive factors actually mean. But they don't. It is these which bring them the most joy.

We may be big and they may be small, but maybe we need to try to see what's small to us more and worry about what's big to us less.

What children want

Children want to feel safe
They want you to smile at them
They want you to hold them
They want you to be there
That costs nothing.

Children want to be happy
They want you to play with them
They want you to laugh with them
They want you to tickle them
That costs nothing.

Children want to be heard
They want you to listen to their cries
They want you to hear their babble
They want you to talk back to them
That costs nothing.

Children want to spend time with you
They want to help you fold the washing
They want to watch you bake a cake
They want you to read a book to them
That costs nothing.

Children want to know that they matter
They want you to talk with your eyes
They want you to get down to their level
They want you to celebrate their milestones
That costs nothing.

Children want to know that you are happy
They want to see your smiles
They want to receive your hugs and kisses
They want to hear your laugh
That costs nothing.

Children want to learn about the world
They want to go for walks with you
They want you to answer their questions
They want you to take the time to explain things
That costs nothing.

Children want to be like you
They want to see how you do things
They want to help you do things
They want to be your shadow
That costs nothing.

Children want you
They want your time
They want your attention
They want your love
That costs nothing.

Today's to-do list

Play with them,
Teach them,
Listen to them,
Console them,
Keep them safe,
Keep them warm,
Keep them fed,
Be present with them,
Enjoy them,
Love them.

If our to-do lists as mothers included the above, we would tick off a lot more each day than we allow ourselves to realise.

And we should.

After all, these "to-dos" are far more important than the state of the dishes, the washing pile or the floor.

They are "productive" and deserve a place at the top of the list.

CHAPTER TWELVE

More than a moment

A picture paints a thousand words, but those thousand words almost never tell the whole story.

Whether the picture be on social media, through the windscreen of your car as you pass a cafe, or through your sunglasses as you engage with other mums at playgroup, the same applies.

When we look at the picture before us, it can be easy to think that some mothers have it all together.
It is just as easy to think some don't seem to have it together.
Unfortunately it seems even easier to judge other mothers in that one moment.

While the pictures can leave an impression on us, it is not the gallery of that mother's journey.

A mother may look immaculate, smile at all times and hold her cards close to her chest, but that doesn't necessarily mean that she always embodies these traits. It may be that she's just had a good night's sleep, is a private person or wanted to wear nice clothes that day.
Her story is more than one moment.

A mother may look disorganised, frazzled and somewhat worn, but that doesn't mean that she always embodies these qualities. It may be that her baby is teething again, that she hasn't had a good night's sleep in weeks or that something happened earlier in the day that rattled her.
Her story is more than one moment.

A mother may let her child have screen time at a cafe while she checks her emails and eats her lunch, but that doesn't mean that she always does this. It may just be that she has deadlines to meet, hasn't eaten since last night or endured tantrums the whole way to the venue.
Her story is more than one moment.

There is ALWAYS more than just one moment.
After all, a day is not made up of only a few seconds, minutes or hours.

It's easy to forget this sometimes when considering the one picture you see.
Perspective can be lost, judgement can unintentionally creep in and unfair weight can be placed on that one frame.
I do it,
We probably all do it sometimes, whether we are aware of it or not.

I often need to remind myself that there is more to a story than just one moment, and I want to remind you of the same.
Don't be so hard on yourself.
Remember,
Your story is always more than one moment.

Stop and see

Overwhelmed Mama,

When you get a moment, stop what you're doing, unclench your
jaw and take a deep breath.
Just stop.
Please just stop.
It's so important to just stop.

Take a look around you. Focus on every bit of the chaos, even the
parts that you would normally try not to see. Zoom in on all the
scattered toys, the crumbs on the couch, and the pile of laundry.
All of that — that mess, that triggering and hard-to-look-at-still-
on-the-to-do-list mess — that's proof of what you have done. It's
your reminder of the fun you have made for your children, the
importance you have placed on them coming first and of how
much you love them.

Then go and look at yourself in the mirror. See yourself completely
though the smudges. Honour her in every sense. Remember all
that she has done for you. Marvel at the pieces of her that look
different, because they are the differences that helped to create the
very people that make her smile every day without having to be
reminded.

Then find your children and hold them tight. See them smile back at you, hold onto you and not let go. Watch them run to you when things don't work and hear them call for you when they're upset. You did that. You made them to start with, and you have now also made them feel safe and content. You have given them the reason to smile and feel that degree of connection.

Then, if you have a partner, call them. Tell them how proud you are of what you are both working hard to create together. Tell them that you appreciate them, and that you cannot wait for them to come home. Wait for them to ask you why you're being so random, then tell them that these sorts of conversations should never be random. They need to happen every day.

Then go and reheat your coffee and carry on with your day. Your chaotic, messy, and never-feels-like-there-is-a-moment kind of day.

And when you do, I promise you that your day will be better. Because you will have allowed yourself a moment to value yourself, your children, and your partner.
Because you will have allowed yourself to see what you are all creating together as a family and the beauty in all the chaos
And all it takes is a moment of just stopping.

Always

You give them what you can, always.
Sometimes it doesn't feel like it's enough.
Sometimes it doesn't feel beautiful.
Sometimes it doesn't feel easy.
But to them, it's everything they need.
It's more than enough.
It's always beautiful.
It's you who gives them ease.

Sometimes it's easy to forget this.
You can feel lost in your own exhaustion.
But they don't let you forget, because to them, you were never lost.
You were always there.
When they were sick.
When they were cold.
When they were scared.

It was you who showed up,
Always.
And it is they who remind you,
Always.

Unasked-for smooches when you are feeling off.
Offerings of crusts after they have eaten.

Towel cuddles after the shower.

These are their offerings of unconditional love, which serve as the important reminder that you are everything they need, want and love.

So they are there for you too,

Always.

It's a beautiful love story.

You both give.

You both take.

And while there are challenges sometimes, each day somewhere amidst it all there is the happy ending you both help write,

Always.

Dearest child,

Tiny lights

You light up the world
With your tiny hands and toes
Your contagious giggles
Your small button nose.

People smile when they see you
They feel immense joy
You take them back to a time
With their own girl or boy.

Siblings, grandparents, uncles
A godparent or cousin
You have the same affect
On one or a dozen.

The joy ripple goes further
It affects strangers too
At the supermarket, the gas station
Coming out of the public loo.

It doesn't matter who you meet
Or the sort of day they've had
Your smile lights them up
They see the good, not the bad.

But you don't know this yet
You're so blissfully unaware
Of your pleasing influence on others
From afar and from near.

For your mothers it's often easier
When they're in a complete rush
To go to town without you
To do the shopping without a fuss.

But it's motivating to remember
Despite the further stress required
The joy your presence can bring
To the young, old and retired.

You are the present and the future
You remind others of their past
Children you light up the world
Forever may it last.

Chapter Thirteen

Dear Guilt-Ridden Mother

Guilt is an emotion wasted on those mothers conscientious enough to care about it.

Careless self-care

To the mother who has gone through yet another day of no proper "self-care", I know what it's like.

I know you're trying. Each morning you promise yourself you will have some time for yourself today. Some days you even tell your husband that he needs to make sure you do it, because you just can't trust yourself to get it done. You read things online that remind you throughout the day that you must make it happen. You deserve it. This is part of being a good mum. It doesn't make you selfish.

But despite your best intentions to read a book, light a candle, do a workout, meditate, paint your nails or have a long bath, it just doesn't happen.

Your self-care looks like sitting in the car and concentrating on the white lines passing underneath you at speed while your child sleeps in the back.

It looks like sitting on the toilet for too long because you haven't heard anything break in the living room since you left.

It looks like sprinting to get your toddler who is halfway down the driveway, or squatting to pick them up at regular intervals because they are having a bad day.

It looks like going to the supermarket alone and sitting in your car at the end of the driveway when you get home, listening to some mindless chat on the radio.

That's the reality of self-care for some of us. And as another day passes, you are hard on yourself for not getting it done.

The guilt you feel is almost as heavy as that which you feel when you do take time for yourself. Almost.

So, you tell yourself tomorrow will be another day, and the cycle starts again.

Recently I have been changing my own narrative. Rightly or wrongly, I tell myself that while as mothers we do need to prioritise self-care, for many of us it's a work in progress.

So, as I sit in the car following a long trip of silence, I am content that for today I have had some time for myself. No, it wasn't my ideal self-care plan and so no, I didn't prioritise myself fully but no, I'm not going to feel guilty about that.

Why?

Because as a mother I feel enough unnecessary guilt every day as it is.

I'm just going to take today as progress because, after all, something is better than nothing.

"I'm a bad mum"

We all say it, right before we confess to something that society considers an inappropriate parenting technique.
"I'm a bad mum because…"

With social media in overdrive and never-ending live workouts, recipes and messy play ideas popping up on our screens, it's no surprise that many of us, by comparison, feel justified in saying we are "a bad mum".

"I'm a bad mum, because I let my child watch television for two hours today."
"I'm a bad mum, because I fed my toddler toast for dinner last night."
"I'm a bad mum, because I didn't make playdough for my little one to play with."
"I'm a bad mum, because I'm not using this time to organise my home."
The list goes on and on and it is nothing new.

Mothers have often prefaced confessions with these four words. There have always been endless lists of what we should and shouldn't do with our children. We read the stories in the media and the posts online, and get constant reminders from everyone about how we should be raising our children.

While there are mothers in society who would be considered by professional standards as "bad mothers" the majority of us who do not fall into this category continue to use this phrase. It seems we are conditioned to do what is "socially acceptable" and in line with the "social norm". If we veer away from either, we often find ourselves justifying why we couldn't or shouldn't have done what we did. It is a way of protecting ourselves from judgement and criticism.

"I'm a bad mum". Whether we think it or vocalise it, we are not doing ourselves or other mothers any favours. We are allowing unfair comparisons to diminish our confidence in our own parenting ability and, in turn, set unhealthy precedents for others.

If you let your child watch television for two hours, you are not a bad mum. You are doing what you need to get some time for yourself or to complete the never-ending list of chores piling up within your four walls.

If you feed your child toast for dinner every now and then, you are not a bad mum. You are doing all you can to survive right now. Simply getting through the day can be tough and, more often than not, all of your proper cooking remains untouched by a picky child anyway.

If you do not make playdough or create sensory-play ideas for your child, you are not a bad mum. You are doing all you can to try and keep yourself and your family happy. We all have different pressures and we must always remember that these varying degrees are not always showcased through social media.

If you do not organise your pantry and linen cupboards, you are not a bad mum. You are prioritising what is important for you and your family right now. We all place value on different things as mothers and, just because our values may be different to others, this does not mean that we are lesser mothers.

We must continue to keep things in perspective, for ourselves, other mothers and our children. If we feel triggered to use this phrase by the state of another mother's immaculate home, amazing meal plans, endless sensory-play ideas and workout regimes, we owe it to ourselves to consider distancing ourselves from them for a bit, whether that be by taking a bit of time off social media, turning to books instead of the web or unfollowing/ muting social media accounts.

If we are doing our best to keep our children, safe, warm, fed and loved, we are amazing mothers. "Bad" doesn't have a place in this context. Don't ever forget it!

My something

I write some days because I need something for me.
I work out some days because I need something for me.
I shout myself a coffee some days because I need something for me.
I hide some of my favourite treats from them because I need
something for me.
I watch Netflix too late because I need something for me.

I do these things because I need something for me.
Just me.
Not my children.
Not my husband.
No one else,
But me.

And I need these somethings because they remind me that I am
still me, that I can still be me, that I am worthy of me.

But most importantly because these somethings make me a better
version of me for them.

And right now, at this point in my life, nothing is more important
to me than them.

Their everything

When you have no energy to give, you give it.
Every ounce of you aches,
Every part of you breaks,
You give everything and more.

When you have no time to spare, you spare it.
Every job becomes bigger,
Every stress spreads wider,
You know what is important.

When you have no positivity to provide, you provide it.
Every smile is forced,
Every moment feels like a test,
Your love knows no limits.

When you have no patience left, you offer it.
Every reaction you try to control,
Everything else can wait,
You handle it.

When you hear their cry, you don't ignore it.
Every emotion runs through you,
Every lost minute of rest doesn't matter,
You rise again.

When you want a break, you don't take it.
Every piece of you feels guilt,
Everyone else is more important,
You carry on.

When you are praised, you don't believe it.
Every criticism you hold onto,
Every compliment is forgotten,
You doubt yourself.

When you see them smile, you don't forget it.
Everything makes sense,
Every part of your being melts,
You are home.

When you have bad days, you should remember,
You are strong,
You are resilient,
You are everything.

When they don't make it easy, don't forget.
They are innocent,
They are vulnerable,
They need everything.

When you doubt whether you are enough, don't question it,
You give everything,
They take everything,
You are their everything.

Unintentional hypocrisy

When a mum tells you she's exhausted, what do you say?

I normally encourage her to take a nap if she can, to take it easy, and I reassure her that it's about surviving not thriving sometimes.
I also normally tell her that I'm tired too, that it's hard and to be gentle on herself.
I don't just say these things to make her feel better.
I mean it, because I believe it.

When a mum tells you she's feeling overwhelmed, what do you say?

I normally suggest she take it day by day, try to prioritise and allow herself to stop and come up for air.
I also normally tell her that my house is a tip, that I often feel overwhelmed and that she's doing a great job.
And I mean it, because I believe it.

When a mum tells you she feels guilty, what do you say?

I normally tell her that I've done the same things, that it's a silly emotion and that she is not alone.
I normally also tell her that I don't know how to beat it, that we all feel it, that she shouldn't be so hard on herself.
And I mean it, because I believe it.

When your inner voice says these same things, what do you tell yourself?

I normally tell myself that I must keep going, that I did enough surviving yesterday, that things cannot wait.
I also normally tell myself to get over it, that some have it worse, that I have no right to complain.
And I believe it, but not because I mean it.

Why?
Why is it hard to give ourselves the same assurances that we offer others?
Why is it that we wait for others to reassure us, rather than reassuring ourselves?
Why are we sometimes so hard on ourselves?

I don't know the why.
I just know the how: What I tell others, I struggle to tell myself.
I rarely day sleep when I'm exhausted.
I don't always take things day by day when I'm overwhelmed.
I am hard on myself when I feel guilty.
I don't just stop and come up for air when needed.
I don't mean to do it, but it happens. It's unintentional hypocrisy, really.
And I pay for it.

So, to those of you in the same boat, remember to offer yourself the same grace, kindness and assurances you do others.
Take the nap, lower the expectations and lose the guilt.
Because Mama, you owe it to yourself.

Stranger

You served us at the grocery store.
You witnessed the tantrum, my offerings of potato chips that we hadn't yet paid for and my eye-rolls when she asked for a different-coloured packet.
You didn't tell me that I should have paid first, or hurry me, or give the "I would have done it differently" look.
You simply said "don't worry, we've all been there".

You were in front of me in the shop queue.
You witnessed me carrying too many things with one hand while trying to keep the pram moving and shush the crying passenger.
You didn't pretend to be checking your phone, or suggest I go and get a trolley, or give me the "control your child" look.
You simply said "I know what that's like, please go in front of me".

You were the barista at the coffee shop.
You witnessed coffee spillage, the sugar sticks being thrown and the screen-time bribery.
You didn't charge me for the second coffee, let me clean up the sugar sticks when I insisted or give me the "that's lazy parenting" look.
You simply said "I wish we had better technology in our day as parents, enjoy your coffee".

You were the older ladies I passed in the street.
You witnessed me pushing an empty pram, carrying a kicking toddler and looking overwhelmed.
You didn't avoid eye contact, exchange whispers or give each other the "should she be holding her child like that?" look.
You simply smiled with your eyes into mine and said "we remember those days, trust us, it does get easier".

You were on the aisle seat opposite us in the aeroplane.
You witnessed me trying to breastfeed awkwardly, walking up and down the aisle regularly and generally just trying everything to stop the baby crying.
You didn't give me an angry stare, turn away from me in obvious protest or give me the "keep your baby quiet" look.
You simply lent over to me and whispered, "it's ok, no one else is worried by it but you".

You are the strangers that make mothers feel supported every day.
Please don't stop.
We need you.

Chapter Fourteen

Dear Lost Mother

She is still there. She will always be there.
She is just taking a break, waiting for you
to be ready to find her again.

Losing yourself

Recently we were in the city
We drove the streets one night
In the car as a family
It was a thought-provoking sight.

The streets were perfectly lit
The restaurants completely packed
I lowered the passenger window
To hear everyone interact.

I could hear glasses clinking
A buzz of excitement in the air
There were women wearing dresses
Makeup on, with straightened hair.

The men were wearing shirts
But drinking beer by the bottle
Some were smoking outside
Others already had the wobbles.

The engagement levels were strong
One's attention rarely diverted
Only to order another drink
Or to check out who'd just flirted.

There was not one pram in sight
No young children causing havoc
No women breastfeeding
Or mothers looking manic.

It took me back to earlier
Post-university, before I was a mum
When going out was enjoyable
We always had so much fun.

For a moment I thought, I pondered
About my different former life
A time when I could do what I wanted
A time when independence was rife.

My dreams were quickly ended
As mum guilt took over my brain
"I am ungrateful to even think that"
"Don't ever think that again!"

The car trip soon concluded
I thought "Gosh, don't be daft"
I'm not a bad mum or ungrateful
I'm allowed to think of the past.

It's part of my history, my story
It makes me the mother I am
I can miss it sometimes, it's natural
It's still part of my life span.

Before motherhood I was someone
During I am someone too
After I'll be another someone
And each stage is worthy of review.

I am Woman

Even if you have all the games in the world, get out for play dates often or have visitors regularly, the days at home can sometimes be long and mundane.

Certainly with younger children many days consist of one-sided conversation and much of the same of, well, just the same as yesterday, last week and last month.

The same favourite books to read, the same washing basket to empty, the same feeding times, the same sleeping times and all within the same four walls.

Counting down the time is not uncommon on these days. Neither is counting down to when your other half is home, to bedtime or just to any chance you have to break the same mundane familiarity that some days consist of.

I used to think that feeling this way made me less of a mother, or ungrateful somehow.
But I'm not.

I'm still a woman who has a brain and craves stimulation by way of adult conversation, just in the way I used to but without needing to seek it out.

I'm still a woman who has personal goals not pertaining to motherhood and looks forward to pockets of time where I can feel that my focus can be diverted there, just in the way I used to but without needing to restrict that time to the one narrow slot called naptime.

I'm still a woman who enjoys socialising and gets excited when there is an opportunity to wear something nice, and drink and eat platters I didn't prepare, just in the way I used to but without needing to worry about what it may mean for my duties the next day.

In my view, just because you crave something other than the sameness of some days in motherhood, doesn't mean anything other than you want to check in with your same old pre-motherhood self. It's that simple.

And I find that when I do, she's right there, thanking me for taking the time to do so and it's just the boost she needs to tackle the next day, which may be the same, but differently.

Water the roots

As a mother, you can sometimes feel like you are losing your brain, but it's important to remember that you are helping grow brand-new ones at the same time.

You will feel yours come back eventually when watered because the roots are already there.
Theirs need to be watered now because the roots need to grow.

Any loss you feel is periodic, but their gains are everlasting. Perspective is everything, always.

Mother Woman

As I looked in the rear-view mirror, there was an empty seat behind me. It was covered in crumbs. The window was marked with finger smudges and the back of the front passenger seat was covered in muddy footprints.

These are the markings of her usual territory, but she wasn't there today. She was being looked after while I did things on my own. It's been a while since I've done this, and I felt completely out of practice.

I had accidentally taken her baby bag with me, even though she wasn't with me.

I often looked in the rear-view mirror to check her while driving, even though she wasn't there to smile back at me.

It took me a while to register that I could use the trolley tray at the grocery store, even though she wasn't perched in it like normal.

I got a grocery treat to take home for her, even though she wasn't there to notice if I ate it on the way home.

She was still at the forefront of my mind, even though she wasn't there.

Before the trip, I couldn't wait to get in the car on my own. I wanted time to do things for myself for a bit, at my pace. I wanted to take my time at the grocery store and attend a workout class in town without the usual disruptions.

I enjoyed it; I did. It was freeing, things were easier, it was what I needed. But it felt a little unusual. It wasn't my new normal.

I felt naked as I walked the streets without her on my hip or holding my hand, in the trolley or in the rear-view mirror.
My mind often wandered. What was she doing? What was she was having for morning tea? I hope she self-settles for her midday nap.

So while I was distanced from her physically, I was still close to her emotionally, in my thoughts and through my behaviours.

That's the thing about being a mother.
Even though you want your own time, you miss them when they're not there.
Even though you don't want to think for a moment about anyone else, you can't help but think about them often.

It's true, you can take the woman out of the mother periodically, but you cannot take the mother out of the woman.
We are changed forever, but in the best way.

Roaring spark

Sometimes I wonder where my spark has gone.

I don't always laugh at jokes like I used to. Probably because I never get the chance to hear the end of them.

The jump in my step is more of a drag right now. Probably because I'm carrying little children, and the heavy load that comes with them.

I don't get as excited about going out as much as I used to. Probably because there's so much involved when taking children. So much to organise and prepare, and then there's the day-after fall out.

I hardly sing along or dance just for the sake of it anymore. Probably because I'm too drained to see the fun in it. The closest I come to letting my hair down is blasting the music in the car when the children aren't in the back seats.

And sometimes I think about my apparent lack of spark. Like when I catch my reflection in everyday life right now. Like when I look in my mirror that still needs a clean, wearing my maternity pants I still wear months after birth, and holding one of my two children who are both still completely dependent on me.

I see a version of myself that is so different than before.
She's so tired, worn, and imperfect.
She screams "In need of a break".
And on the face of it, the spark isn't easy to see.

But truth be told, this version of her is by far the most content, loved, and free she has ever been.
And the spark is still there.
In fact, there is so much more spark to this woman than ever before.

Now all of her sparks are combined at her core.
They roar deep within, underneath the misleading layers of her exterior and behaviours.
They're the limitless love she has for them. The burning desire to be better for them, to do better for them and to be and do all she can to help them shine bright.

Because they are her spark.
Because they make her spark.
Because she wants them to feed off her spark and shine brightest of all.

And as I go to leave the mirror smudges for another day, I'm reminded of this as my baby smiles at me, my current reflection, more brightly than ever.
And I feel the spark to my core.

I'm reminded that it's still there,
Even if I can't see it some days.

Dearest child,

nothing compares

I could walk for hours in the most scenic of settings, but your smile will always be the best view.
Even though it may be short-lived,
Even though I hardly see it some days,
It is a beauty like no other.

I could enjoy the finest of wines and cheeses, but the leftover crusts you offer me will always taste best.
Even though they are rock hard and covered in slobber,
Even though they do not fill me up,
They signify your love for me.

I could sit in nature for hours listening to her peaceful soundtrack, but your laugh is the best sound I will ever hear.
Even though it is sometimes at my expense,
Even though it may only be the break between cries,
It is the best medicine.

I could spend years looking for the perfect jewel, but the sparkle in your eye is the jewel no money can buy.
Even though I won't always be the first to see it,
Even though others will try and dull it,
It is priceless.

I could grind away to reach all of my career goals, but hearing you say "I love you Mum" will always give me the best sense of fulfilment.
Even though there is no certificate,
Even though you may not always say it,
Once in a lifetime is enough.

I could seek validation from everyone else about my parenting, but you crying for me is the only validation that matters.
Even though it frustrates me sometimes,
Even though it makes me extremely tired,
You matter most.

I love you, my child.

A future letter

To my children reading this one day,

You were one of the best things to happen to me.
I talked about it being hard because it was.
It was relentless.
There was never really a moment to stop. There was always
something and someone else to worry about. I worried so much
for you.
And there was always more to do, most that did not get done.
That was hard.
But loving you wasn't.
Nothing has ever come easier.

You gave me so much joy and purpose, during a time in my life
that I could so often feel lost.
I would feel my old life moving further and further away, but you
would bring me closer than ever to where I needed to be.
You became my life, for many years.
You will forever be one of the biggest parts of my life.
But you have your own now.
And I have parts of mine back, as well as new parts I often
dreamed of and planned with you at my feet, or on my hip and
lap, or late at night with you in my arms.
You helped me find the new.

You are the reason I got here.
You were always my why.

And I miss you. I miss your littleness, your dependence, your chaos.
I miss being the first person you come to when things go wrong, and the last person you see at night.
I miss the mess that drove me up the wall, and your gravitation to me rather than the ground and the space around us.
I remember the beauty like it was yesterday. Because it was beautiful. You are beautiful.
And all the hard?
I forgot about that when you left.

And I just want you to know,
That even though we no longer share the same roof, or bed, or everything including time, please remember I'm just a phone call away. I'll always answer for you, no matter the time or the size of the problem.
But there doesn't need to be a problem. Please just call.
Because I'm still here for you.
Because I'll always be your mum.
Because you will always be my babies.

Love Mum x

CHAPTER FIFTEEN

DEAR LONELY MOTHER

You can be busy interacting with little humans all day and still feel lonely. It's ok to feel like this. You are still a good mother.

Connected by motherhood

You may not have known each other for that long, in fact, you may have only just met, but that doesn't matter.

Through sunken eyes and unforgiving yawns, you try to exchange stories in the stop-start fashion you have each become accustomed to.

Through unrelenting background noises and the constant "Mum, Mum, Mum", you try to maintain eye contact with each other but forever fall short.

Through little tugs from below and meddling fingers at your hip, you try to finish the coffees you have been looking forward to all morning.

And when things turn pear-shaped, as they often do, you both part ways with unfinished stories, connection and coffee.

But that's ok.
Because while you may be unsure when you will meet again to finish the unfinished, or indeed to start right back at the beginning,
You both just get it,
And sometimes that's all that matters.

Knowledge is power

Sometimes you cannot relate to another mother's experience and, in that moment, you can feel alone.
"Why don't they feel the same way?"
"Am I the only one who feels like this?"
"What do they do that I don't?"

No one likes feeling alone but know that you are not.
Your inability to relate to one mother's overall experience with motherhood doesn't mean that you won't relate to another mother's experience.
In the same way that your inability to relate to one mother's first stage of motherhood doesn't mean that you won't relate to their second, third or fourth stage.

That's the thing about motherhood.
While individually our journeys are different, collectively we travel to the same destination: The pursuit of happiness, for ourselves, our children and our families.
And as you travel in that one-way direction, the traffic is always heavy. The sheer numbers alone mean that there will always be someone else who is going through or who has gone through what you are.

You may meet them in your travels; you may never.
You might read their story, you may listen to their podcast or you may watch their online videos while travelling.
But they are out there in the traffic with you now, or have been out there before.

So, whether you are enjoying every moment, struggling to see the light, or somewhere in between, your experience is not yours to feel alone in and remembering that can be powerful.

Dearest child,

There you are

There you are,
Looking at me as if I am everything you dreamed of. Your kind of perfection. Naive to my insecurities and weaknesses.
Soaking me in, unconditionally.

There you are,
Right in my space, without any desire to be elsewhere. Your safe place. Unaware that you are mine too.
Holding on to me, not letting go.

There you are,
Fighting sleep as if you never want our time together to end. Your nightmare. Unintentionally teaching me to see the battle for what it is.
Your enjoyment of our time, of us.

There you are,
Messing up the clean, thinking you are "helping". Your little contribution. Testing me to work on my weaknesses, to embrace imperfect.
You are helping me, to grow.

There you are,
Reaching for me with tears streaming down your face, as if I am
your only cure. Your resolute saviour. Blind to the crowd of people
around you.
Seeing only me, for now.

There you are,
Smiling when your dad and I hug, as if it's the best sight in the
world. Your world. Not yet knowing that you are our entire
universe, and more.
You're our star in the night and sun in the rain.

There you are,
Teaching me, reminding me, helping me grow.
Doing more than you can understand just yet, and more than I
can see some days.

Thanks for being there,
I needed you too.
Please just stay for a while.

Live it longer

One day we'll sit together and you will ask me about this time. We will peruse the old photos of us, and talk about the stage of life you won't remember a lot of but which I'll never be able to forget. The beautiful and chaotic stage of little hands and feet, of big mess and emotions.

I'll look different to the photos by then, time having aged me. You'll probably comment on my then hair colour, or laugh at my then style, or tell me how young I looked back then.
And I'll laugh too. And defend myself. And compare me now to me then.
Because that's what it's all about.

And then I'll tell you more.

I'll tell you that this was then, this was me, this was us. You were that small and I was that young.

I'll tell you that we lived here in this house, in this kitchen, in each other's arms. I held you like this and watched you like that.

I'll tell you that when this photo was taken, you had been running circles around me all day and I was tired. I was always tired. You loved to be busy, but it kept me on my toes.

I'll tell you that we shared many one-sided stories at the sink, or the bath, or anywhere really. And tears, and laughter. It was all easier then, even though it felt harder.

I'll tell you things about yourself that you didn't already know, and I'll be the first to admit that I was not perfect. But I was there for you. We were there for each other.

I'll tell you that these were the best days. Of us at home, doing everything some days and nothing other days. It all went too fast.

I may not think to tell you, but I'll want to relive this.
I'll want to go back to just us. To be more than an afterthought.
But I won't be able to.
So I will take you back there with me, with my photos, and my stories and my memories triggered by all of the little things I keep to remind me of this time.

We will relive it, together.
One day.
But for now, let me live it longer.

Chapter Sixteen

Dear Mother Wife

You will have less time with your partner,
but spending time as a family becomes what you crave.

Pulled apart

Through the door he comes
It's after 5 o'clock
"Where have you been?" I ask
My stomach in a knot.

I don't wait for him to tell me
I just hurry him inside
"Please bath them, help me, now!"
There is no time for pride.

I direct him to their needs
A weight lifted from my day
Help, finally, at last
I'm not sure what else to say.

I don't ask about his work
Or see the tired in his eyes
I just see him as my lifeline
After a day full of cries.

They gravitate towards him
Arms outstretched; eyes wide
Their way of telling him
"Mum has become a little tired".

I can't help but notice
Their smiles are just for him
I wonder where mine have gone
And then I pour a gin.

He goes about his business
While I go about mine
Both of us making it through
The hard before bedtime.

I pass him in the hallway
Sit next to him during tea
Yet I'm still far too distracted
By the littles on our knees.

It's not until it's quiet
And I see him at the sink
Still in his work clothes; helping
His tired is at the brink.

I wonder how his day has been
Did he see a lot of good?
Or did he leave feeling defeated?
Perhaps now he understood.

Sometimes I don't ask him
The answers left in the dark
Waiting for the next day
I'm not completely pulled apart.

But when I'm pieced together
I meet him at the sink
I ask him how his day has been
In the first moment I've had to think.

Invisible

You can be invisible to each other.
Even though you're both there, it's hard to see each other through the little ones in between.

It's easy to forget that you each have your own needs and needs to each other when you're in the thick of it. You can be in the same room for hours and not see each other through the chaos, or in the car for long trips but not hear each other through the noise.
The focus of your attention is rarely on each other anymore.

While you're packing the car frantically because you're running late, you forget to tell them how nice they look in their new shirt and they forget to tell you that they like your hair like that.

While you're sorting the children and they're trying to get out the door for work you forget to wish them well for their big day and they forget to give you a kiss goodbye.

While you message them about the baby wipes or the money you need transferred, you forget to ask how their day is going and they forget to click send on their reply.

While you complain to each other about being tired or needing a break, you forget to do that important thing for them and they forget to use your favourite mug when making your coffee.

While you chew their ear off about what you did all day and they can't wait to tell you about an upcoming boys' trip, you forget to hear the importance of each other's needs, just the impact on your own.

And as you leave an empty space in the bed to have some you time while they spend time with the children, you forget to tell them how grateful you are for them, and they forget to tell you how much they appreciate you.

Parenting.
It can make you forgetful and blind. You forget to see each other some days and it can feel like you are connected through some form of disconnection.

Even so, it's one of the most fulfilling chapters you'll go through together. And when you remember to see each other for yourselves and what you both are for the little ones in between, even for the shortest time, it leaves your heart feeling full and your connection feeling the deepest it's been for the longest time.
Until next time,
When, once again, you need to remember to see.

A new love language

As I opened the door after a weekend away, my heart warmed.
The floors were vacuumed, the bench was wiped and the toys were
put away.
It was a beautiful sight, but it's more than that, so much more.

I didn't ask him to do it; he just did it.
It's not always like this, but when it is, it's like a romantic gesture
of sorts.
Since becoming a mum, this is what gives me the butterflies and
warm heart.

For me, it's not about roses, chocolates or romantic dinners,
it's about having the washing folded, the lawns mown or the
dishwasher emptied when I least expect.
It's not about being taken away for long weekends, it's about him
taking them for a while so I can catch up on sleep, with the house,
with work, with myself.
It's not about being told I look great in a dress or shoes or makeup,
but being told I am doing a good job at being a mum.
Because that's what I appreciate most now.

Flowers and chocolates are nice, of course they are, but flowers
and chocolates do not help me day to day, give me a rest or a
slightly shortened to-do list.

Weekends away are amazing, but they do not help with the work emails, the sleep, the state of the house.

Being told I look nice is flattering, but that is not what matters most to me right now. What matters is them, the happiness of our family, and surviving.

Some may think this is lowering expectations. "He should do that for you anyway", "you should still have time for you", "you should still get the flowers and the chocolates, the weekends away".

But for me, it's not about lowering expectations. He still does these things (sometimes), we still do these things (sometimes), it's just that our expectations have changed because the context has.

From just the two of us, to us as a family.

From the husband and wife to the mum and dad.

And our values have been amended too, naturally.

It's always been about recognising what we both appreciate and giving that, it's just that now what we appreciate is a little different.

For me, it's the things that make me feel seen, heard and appreciated in the current chapter of motherhood that matter most.

That's the new love language.

Leftovers

The leftovers are for him.
The pieces of me that remain, in some way or form, but are not
really that whole.
The main meal having been dined on by our little ones
throughout the day.

He gets the side plate of my energy, love and mental space.
The nibbled-at pieces, the crusts, the smaller portion.
They are not always the best bits.
Some of the worst, in fact.

Of course, I'd love for him to have more of the best, the fresh, the
substance.
And even though he says leftovers taste best anyway,
He would too, I'm sure.
It's just that some days it feels like there isn't enough to go around.

But the point that I often forget is that I do try and leave some of
me aside for him every day,
No matter if served slightly cold or left for another day.
I do, because I know he needs me too,
And sometimes, it's just the thought that counts.

Dearest husband,

I haven't forgotten

I haven't forgotten.
I haven't forgotten who we were, what we were or the life we led.
It's still there, in the back of my mind.
And it moves forward whenever I see an old photo of us
somewhere, hidden between those of them.

I think back to that life.
Of how young and carefree we were.
Of us being everything and anything to each other.
Of us living and breathing what we wanted, when we wanted and
how we wanted.

I think about the Sunday morning lie-ins and the freedom we
had to explore things in our own time, in each other's time, in the
seemingly endless time.
It was so different.
We were so different.

You used to be the first one I'd see in the morning and the last one
I'd see at night.
The comfort was only ours to have.
And there was such comfort in that. In knowing that.
In everything about that.

Now the comfort is spread.
It's most often found with them, and for them.
Every morning, every night and every moment in between.
And that's how it should be.
We come second right now.
To them, and to each other.
And I wouldn't change a thing.

But I haven't forgotten, and I won't ever forget, the life before this
life.
Of the two of us, before them.
Of the ups and downs, the constant.
Of our love, which came first.

One day we will again converse in full sentences, wake only to the
sounds of each other and have the other's hand free to hold.
And one day our eyes will again meet more often, our shoulders
will touch when we sit on the same couch and we will talk at
length with all the time we have about missing the empty spaces
between us.

But until then, know that I haven't forgotten.
That part of our life is what got us here, and got us them.
It matters,
And so do you.

Saying it

I know I don't say it sometimes, but I'm grateful for you.
You carry more than them on your shoulders, even though some days that feels enough.
You carry me when I need it, even when I don't know I do.
You help carry us as a family, sometimes making me forget how heavy the load can be.

I know I don't say it sometimes, but I see you.
You work hard every day so I can be home, even when your sleep is broken.
You are home when needed so I can have a break, even when there is more work to do.
You are present as a father and a husband, sometimes making me forget how lucky I am.

I know I don't say it sometimes, but I'm here for you too.
When you are tired and tapped out. I know it's not a competition, even if I make it seem like one.
When you are stressed and overwhelmed. I know how hard you are working, even though I may not acknowledge it.
When you need a break and some space. I know how much it's needed; sometimes let me carry you too.

I know I don't say it sometimes, but thank you.

For the way you are with them as a father and me as a mother.

For everything you are and for everything you do.

For sharing the load, always.

I know I don't say it sometimes, but I love you.

Chapter Seventeen

Dear Motherhood

You can be a hard gig, but you open up minds, feed souls and fill up the hearts of those who have the privilege of experiencing you.

What she thought she knew

She thought she would sit in a cafe for hours while her baby napped, while she drank coffee and chatted with her friends.

She thought that she would have time to keep the house tidy and the gardens immaculate while her toddler played on a mat surrounded by toys and snacks.

She thought she would prepare all meals from scratch, make packed lunches and always have frozen meals in the freezer.

She thought she would be out late at night for dinner and at long lunches with her friends while her children moulded in with her life completely.

She thought that she would fit into her old clothes in the same way, have time to work out on her terms and have a neat mum wardrobe filled with fashionable activewear and pearly white sneakers.

She thought wrong because she didn't know.

She now knows that she can only sit in a cafe for half an hour at best before a wake, a spill, or a tantrum. She buys takeaway coffee while dining in (just in case), any food she attempts to eat is cold or shared, and any chat is short-lived.

She now knows that she can garden and clean, but only when her children nap, only IF her children nap, and any self-occupation/ time on the mat is fleeting with a toddler, no matter the variety of snacks and toys.

She now knows that feeding her children processed food and bought lunches is sometimes necessary and generally the only things "frozen" are the vegetables she puts on the side of the plate for balance.

She now knows that going out late at night or for long lunches is a bad idea because naptime is the worst time to be out in a overstimulating environment with young children.

She now knows that most of her pre-mum clothes are not worth keeping, workouts are never fully on her terms, and her wardrobe is largely made up of nothing white and everything comfort over style.

And she knows this now, because this is based on what she lives every day in real life,
Not what she lives through momentarily online.

Real motherhood

Real motherhood is often what's behind the social media feeds, the small talk at coffee groups and the closed doors of the four walls.

It's wanting them to go to sleep at night, because you're completely spent. Too spent to put the toys away, or the dishes away, or the wash on at night. And that annoys you.

It's seeing your other half go to work or away for a weekend. You say it's fine, but it doesn't feel fine. You want to have that sort of freedom, even for a moment. To just drop things and leave without a care in the world, or a baby bag.

It's losing it over the small things like the beeping dishwasher or the lost remote when you are so sleep deprived you cannot control your eyelids, let alone your mood. Most of the time, losing it has nothing to do with these things.

It's feeling alone and craving some adult discussion. To get away for a moment and feel like you can still speak in full sentences. Ironically, almost all discussions are about them when you do.

It's feeling like you have lost your mind by 5pm at the latest every day, and wondering if it will ever come back again one day, let alone by morning.

It's wanting to be on your own sometimes, to have your coffee, your breakfast, or so much as your body to yourself for even a minute.

This is the "some of the time" in real motherhood.
And like all things, there needs to be the "some" making up the "all".

The "all of the time" in motherhood is loving them so damn much that you cannot remember life before them, or imagine what you would do without them or what your life would be if something ever happened to them. It hurts too much to think about that, but you do sometimes.

It's knowing the privilege of being someone's everything, every day for years, and then breaking at the thought of it ending. But it always will someday. The years go far too fast.

It's feeling like it's all worth it every day without question, no matter what. No matter how hard, how lonely or how mundane it can feel some of the time.

It's knowing that you would never trade this chapter for sleep, for the world, for anything.

And thankfully, that's real too.
That's real motherhood.
All of it.

Their first

I'm the last.

I'm the last to have breakfast,
To get myself dressed,
To brush my teeth.

And I'm the last to get out the door,
To buy something for myself,
To sit down for a moment.

And I'm the last to have a shower,
To turn off the lights,
To fall asleep every night.

But I'm also the first.

The first they run to when they're excited,
The first they cry for when they're upset,
The first they come to for everything.

So I may come last because they come first,
But I also come first because I am their first,
And it's just nice to remember that some days.

Contradiction

Motherhood is wondering whether you're doing enough, despite being more than enough.

It's feeling lonely sometimes, despite always being in the best company.

It's trying to find yourself, despite never actually losing yourself.

It's the constant pulls from below, despite the mental push from above.

It's reading everything, despite rarely following anything.

It's feeling out of control, despite being in control.

It's being selfless most of the time, despite craving selfishness some of the time.

It's running on an empty tank most days, despite overflowing with love every day.

It's nothing you thought it would be, despite being so much more than you ever thought it could be.

Motherhood.
Despite it all,
It's everything.

Deep

I've always been an emotional person, but since I've become a mother I cry at the drop of a hat.
About everything.
And anything.
Including things that have absolutely nothing to do with me but make me think of my children.
Particularly things that make me realise how quickly they will be no longer be children.
Certainly, things that remind me of how lucky I am that they are healthy, and safe, and with us.
And always things that make me go into their rooms at night and kiss them again when they are asleep, or find them and hold them for the longest time when they are awake, or take them in the shower with me when they have already had a bath, because I want them close.

Some of the reaction is due to being tired and hormonal, but most of it is due to feeling so deeply because I love so deeply now.
And because I'm so grateful, and worried for them.
Because they are everything to me and my heart is vulnerable for them.
They have cracked me open.
My heart is forever outside of my chest, exposed to all that they are.

So, when I'm reminded of how much they really do mean, of what really is at stake, and what really is not worth worrying about, my heart bursts, and my tears fall.
They probably always will now,
Because this kind of love is deep.
And I'm in deep,
Tears and all.

Big little needs

I'll never be needed this much again.

I won't have to spend my minutes and hours, days and nights, weekends and holidays being someone's constant.

I won't have to eat every meal in record time, reheat my coffee every morning or hide treats in the highest of shelves.

I won't have to ignore the dirty mirrors, the crumbs in the car, or the state of my nails.

I won't have to use the bathroom with a crowd, brush my teeth while dancing to the Wiggles, or shower with the door open.

I won't have little hands and feet touching every part of me when I feel touched out, or big emotions crashing into me when I feel like I've crashed.

I won't have to stop everything I start, restart everything I've stopped, or apologise for running late, again and again.

I won't have to answer hundreds of questions, google many of the answers, or pretend that hearing the same sentence over and over is still surprising.

I won't have to do everything one handed, take far too long to leave the house or lug around a huge baby bag.

I won't have to answer their calls in the middle of the night to calm fears, or feed comfort, or simply lie there with them.

I won't have to wake before I'm ready, or try to sleep after I'm woken, or be tired every moment.

Because the need right now,
The exhausting, intense, relentless, and all-consuming need,
It's not forever.
It's just now,
Right now.
And the right now will eventually fade into the time that I cannot keep up with,
Like it always does in this season.

And one day it will be a different need.
A lesser, more distant need.
A need they don't always ask for or accept.
One of needing to be picked up from a party, of needing money for a new car, or of thinking they "don't need to talk about it" to anyone, including to me.
And that will be hard, and confusing, I'm sure.
And I'll want to be needed, just as I am right now, all over again.

So while I'm here, right now, having never been so drained from being so needed in all my life, I'm reminding myself that I'll also never be needed this much or in this way, ever again in my life.
And I'm holding onto them and their big needs a little tighter.

Still

When things go wrong I still think of her.
I want to call her and tell her.
I want her reassurance, and advice.

She's sometimes the first person I want to hear on the other end of
the phone.
Please answer.
Please answer.
And she's also the last person I want to feel my pain.
Don't make her worry.
Don't make her worry.

But I call her anyway.
Because I know she will want to help.
And I know she will worry anyway.
The worry never stops.
But neither does the pull.

I still gravitate to her.
Even though we're apart.
Even though all these years have passed.
Even though I'm an adult and I have my own children, husband,
and life to worry about.

"I want to call mum".

These are the words that came after some bad news.

And they made me realise.

I still need her.

I will probably always still need her.

Sometimes, somewhere, somehow.

And I love that.

Because it means that maybe, just maybe, my children will always need me too.

I get it now

I get it now.

I get why she has more photos of us than anyone else down the hallway.

I get why she kept some of our little baby clothes, shoes and toys stored away after she finished having children.

I get why Father Christmas still visited us in our teens.

I get why she kept our rooms set up for years after we left.

I get why our school reports and certificates still have their own folders in her filing cabinet.

I get why the reminders on the fridge are often covered by old memorabilia of us.

I get why our favourite children's books still have a place on her bookshelves.

I get why some of our childhood art remains on her kitchen wall.

I get it now.

We were her why.

Dear Motherhood

You are the hardest, most exhausting, confusing and heart-wrenching thing to ever happen to me,
But you are also by far the best thing to ever happen to me.
I'm so glad I took a chance on you.

Sincerely,
Emma Heaphy.

You can find me on:

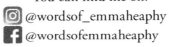 @wordsof_emmaheaphy

@wordsofemmaheaphy

Printed in Great Britain
by Amazon